Portuguese-Hawai'i
KITCHEN

The *Local Foods* of *Island Portuguese*

WANDA A. ADAMS

Photography by
Ian Gillespie
&
Kaz Tanabe

Mutual
Publishing

Star ★ Advertiser

For Grandma and Mom
Abencao, Vovo e Mamae

I beg your blessings today as you gave so freely
of your skill and wisdom in days past.

Library of Congress Control Number: 2014936344

ISBN: 978-1939487-09-4

Recipe photography by Ian Gillespie, except as noted below
Photography by Kaz Tanabe: pg. 6-20, 27, 30, 33
Art direction by Jane Gillespie
Cover design by Jane Gillespie
Interior design by Courtney Tomasu
Portuguese plates provided by Filipe Robelo

First Printing, August 2014
Second Printing, September 2019

Mutual Publishing, LLC
1215 Center Street, Suite 210
Honolulu, Hawai'i 96816
Ph: 808-732-1709 / Fax: 808-734-4094
email: info@mutualpublishing.com
www.mutualpublishing.com

Printed in South Korea

Photos on page xviii, 65 courtesy of Duarte family
Photos on page 4-5, 21, 23, 37, 57, 74, 91, 187 by Wanda A. Adams
Photos on page 155, 179 by Carl E. Koonce III
Photos on page 45, 116 © Hawai'i State Archives
Photo on page 129 by Dean Sensui
Top photo on page 143 courtesy *Mid-Pacific Magazine*
Photo on page 148 courtesy of the Tavares family and Bishop Museum
Photo on page 169 © *Honolulu Star-Advertiser*
Photos from Dreamstime.com:
pg. ii © Madrabothair, pg. iii (paper) © Ira0109, pg. xi (tile background), 63, 83, 147, 188 © Rui Caldeira, pg. v © Pablo Caridad, pg. xvii © Vlntn, pg. xviii (photo frame) © Tim Hester, pg. xix © Christian Draghici, pg. 1 © Incomible, pg. 39 © Ti_to_tito, pg. 42 © Steven Cukrov, pg. 43 © Lepas, pg. 44 © Slavica Mladenovic, pg. 47 © Carlos Caetano, pg. 48 © Joseph Gough, pg. 50 © Jianghongyan, pg. 53 © Robert Paul Van Beets, pg. 75 © Denali55, pg. 79 © Margouillat, pg. 94 © Sarah Marchant, pg. 114 © Homydesign, pg. 126 © Tiagoladeira, pg. 143 (bottom) © Sergiy Palamarchuk, pg. 146 © Ang Hui Hoen, pg. 149 © Antonio Gravante, pg. 157 © Jumnong, pg. 160 © Nilabarathi, pg. 163 © Juan Moyano, pg. 167 © Mats Honkamaa, pg. 178 © Ppy2010ha, pg. 181 © Italianestro, pg. 182 © Anke Van Wyk, pg. 185 © AGLphotoproductions, pg. 195 © Jerryb8, pg. 201 © Nataliya Evmenenko

Star ★ Advertiser

A Portuguese-Hawai'i Kitchen was the second in a series from Mutual Publishing and the *Honolulu Star-Advertiser* exploring Hawai'i's many ethnic cuisines.

Wanda Adams, former food editor for the *Honolulu Advertiser* and the author of five cookbooks, celebrates her heritage and her family with this personal collection of recipes handed down from generation to generation.

This book is a tribute to her grandmother and mother—a culinary history of their hard work and their collective memories of traditional Portuguese cuisine and how it became part of Hawai'i's local table. The recipes reach far beyond well-known favorites such as Portuguese Bean Soup and malasadas—you'll come away with a better understanding and appreciation for Portuguese cooking methods, traditions, and flavors.

At the *Honolulu Star-Advertiser* we celebrate the diversity of island cuisine every week on our Food pages. We are proud to build on that tradition with the series "Hawai'i Cooks."

Dennis Francis
President and publisher,
Honolulu Star-Advertiser and Oahu Publications Inc.

CONTENTS

Temperos e Salsas
SEASONINGS, SAUCES AND BASE RECIPES

Aperitivos e De Manha
FIRST COURSES AND FIRST MEALS

Sopas
soups

Carnes e Aves
MEATS

Peixes, Mariscos e Mollusca
FISH, SHELLFISH, MOLLUSKS

Grao, Milho, Arroz, Feijão
GRAINS, CORNMEAL, RICE, BEANS

Salades e Legumes
SALADS, VEGETABLES

O Pão
BREAD

Doces
SWEETS

APPENDICES

Obrigada
I AM OBLIGATED

Thank you to everyone who helped: home cooks who shared recipes with me, and community cookbooks that jogged my memory or inspired me to creation (especially the works of the Portuguese Heritage Council, Chef John Peru, the Maui Home Extension Homemakers Council and Hawaiian Electric).

Thanks for five months of joyful work to the chefs and experts who provided the recipes and knowledge for this book's new chapter and gave of their time for photos and talk story. Mahalo piha to my old friend Daniel Leung, program coordinator for the Kapiʻolani Community College Culiinary Arts Department, and his wife, Jenny, who loaned us their cook's paradise of a home kitchen for the new chapter photo shoot.

Obrigada to Laura Figueroa and Sandy Tsukiyama for assistance with Portuguese language.

Most of all, my love and respect to the elders who protested they knew nothing and then talked for hours about old days and old ways.

Finally, to the publisher, the editors and the creative team at Mutual Publishing who encouraged me to revise and update this book and were patient with She Who Cannot Meet a Deadline.

THE HAWAI'I COOKS SERIES

This series is not meant to be a guide to the "traditional" cooking of any ethnic group. You can find those cookbooks in any bookstore. These books are a reflection of the various cuisines as they have developed—deliciously—in our islands.

The writers are a mixed group, united by the fact that they grew up in Hawai'i, learning from their parents and grandparents, aunties and uncles, to cook the dishes of their heritage, but local-style.

There is a difference. Each immigrant group arrived in the islands over a set period of years, with eating habits that reflected those of the homeland at that time. Back in Asia or Portugal, meanwhile, cuisine grew and changed. This evolution worked both ways. In Hawai'i, cooks adapted traditional dishes to local ingredients. And as circumstances improved, they used more of the sugar and meat that became affordable to them.

End result: Today a visitor from Japan might find our Japanese food recognizable but sweet; a Korean might be surprised by the amount of meat on the typical Korean menu; someone from Portugal might wonder, what is this thing we call Portuguese Bean Soup?

The heritage is to be respected, the differences to be celebrated, the deliciousness simply to be enjoyed.

The *Hawai'i Cooks* series includes Korean, Okinawan, Chinese, Filipino, and Japanese cuisines.

DIG IN.

Betty Shimabukuro and Muriel Miura
Editors

PREFACE

Any cookbook writer will tell you: The moment the book is published, you want it back. You learn more, you meet new mentors. And, of course, you are blessed with more recipes.

So I am more than delighted that Mutual Publishing invited me to revise, update and add a new chapter to the original 2014 edition of *A Portuguese Kitchen.*

The new chapter visits the worlds of chefs, travelers to Portugal and Brazil and home cooks who delight in the food of Lusitana (the Roman province that became Portugal).

Portuguese cooking is very, very simple. That's what makes it so tricky. It requires the freshest, most flavorful ingredients, a confident understanding of a few crucial techniques and a visceral approach (look, listen, smell, taste, touch throughout the process). Do not be impatient. Much of this cooking is a long, slow process of building flavor and texture. Active preparation time is often short but actual cooking time can take days.

The long, slow approach is because much of this rustic food was the work of busy, stay-at-home women with large families, who tucked their cooking tasks between other chores: stirring a pot, tasting, adjusting the heat, adding ingredients and extracting others. Mostly though, the soups, stews, braises and marinated foods that form the heart of this cuisine tend themselves.

This book is the work of many, many work-worn hands, mine only the most recent of them. It is primarily a work of culinary history: stories of interesting characters and dishes entwined with recipes. These dishes date to a time when most Portuguese burned thousands of calories a day in manual labor. While I trimmed fat and sugar where it could be done with no ill effect, or would make the dish appeal better to to-day's tastes, these recipes are much as they were given to me.

One of the most exciting things about researching the new chapter was learning new techniques for familiar dishes; seeing how narrow my view was of Portuguese cooking for so long, limited to my grandmother's kitchen. Revolutionary idea: Your Grandma's or Grandpa's ways weren't the only ways.

Obrigada, my cooking mothers and fathers. I, and they, hope you will use their legacy recorded on these pages to teach your children and grandchildren the Portuguese way.

—*Wanda Adelaide Adams*
(Duarte, Sylva clans)
Kalihi, 2019

INTRODUCTION
PORTUGUESE AT THE TABLE

I'm often asked why Hawai'i has had so few Portuguese restaurants. Like, two, that I know of: One that existed in the '60s or '70s, called Lisboa, and Adega, which opened in 2012 in Chinatown.

My answer has been a shrug. And sometimes I say, kidding but kind of meaning it, too, that Portuguese elders were too thrifty to pay for something at a restaurant that they could make at home. A better answer is probably that Portuguese intermarried so freely and ac-culturated so rapidly—largely losing their language, fledgling Portuguese schools and many customs—that few were living Portuguese-style by mid-20th century.

Still, I was intrigued by the ques-tion of restaurants, and many others I had about Portuguese Hawai'i food, and that was the seed of this book, planted more than a decade ago. I began to research Portuguese recipes in the oldest cook-books I could find, and I took enough conversational Portuguese that, coupled with my grade-school Spanish, I could flounder my way through microfiche of lo-cal Portuguese newspapers in the Hawai'i State Library.

There were, between 1885 and 1927, a dozen such newspapers, some published on O'ahu and some in Hilo, according to a 1961 paper by Edgar C. Knowlton, "The Portuguese Language Press of Hawai'i." But they had no food pages, despite advertisements for goods of interest such as dried beans, olive oil and Portuguese wines.

U Uniao Lusitana, a Honolulu-based Portguese newspaper from 1894.

Community cookbooks were great for tracking changes in the post-war years. At first, there were many types of Portuguese recipes, but, gradually, that faded into the Predictable Five: pão doce (sweetbread), sopas feijoa (bean soup), vinha d'ahlos (pickled pork), linguiça (sausage) and malassadas (doughnuts). Unfortunately, few island cookbooks were published prior to the 1940s, and those that were available were not written for the likes of Maria Tunta.

The elite considered Portuguese food too rustic and highly spiced. It was the era of cream sauce and mayonnaise, not garlic and tomatoes.

This belies the influence that Portuguese immigrants had on Hawai'i, as they did on the culinary histories of every continent. It has been said that the Portuguese voyagers gave Koreans chili powder; Japanese deep-frying techniques, sweet potatoes and sponge cakes; Okinawans andagi, Hawaiians chilies (thus influencing such key dishes as lomi salmon and poke).

The Portuguese Atlantic Islands, like Hawai'i, grew sugar cane, pineapple, bananas, avocado, mango, guava, figs, passion fruit, papaya, all manner of citrus, and sweet potatoes. Fish, particularly tuna, octopus, bonito and marlin, were the "meat" of even the poor. Every house kept pigs and chickens. Cattle were scarce due to a lack of pastureland, but beef was greatly appreciated.

Additionally, however, there was a world of herbs and spices little known in the islands—chilies, bay laurel, cilantro, mint, flat-leaf parsley, rosemary, garlic, marjoram, oregano. And, in place of poi, there was bread, rice and cornmeal. All these would travel with immigrants in carefully tended little pots, treasured envelopes of seeds, cloth bags of hoarded grains.

This book catalogs the foodways of this vibrant community and the many contributions the Portuguese have made to the islands' mixed plate. My best information has come from oral histories, both those in libraries and at the UH Oral History Center and those I've taken myself, from Portuguese elders. You'll meet some of them, and some of their ingredients, in essays sprinkled throughout this book.

Venha conmigo.
COME WITH ME.

VOVÔ, A CULINARY TRIBUTE

Family, church, kitchen and garden. These were my grandmother's life. Her name was Adelaide "Ida" Sylva Duarte, and she was as sweet and wholesome as a new-season apple. As practical as a farmer. As patient as a saint. As cute as a kitten (given to blushing, giggling and talking baby talk). And as efficient and organized as an accountant. Her most daring swear words were "Oh ... sugar!"

Because my mother was a career woman in partnership in various businesses with my father, I spent my days and many nights at Grandma and Grandma's sprawling Maui homes, first in Wailuku and then in 'Iao Valley. For a few years Grandma and and I shared a bedroom; I would fall asleep to the susurration of her saying her rosary. (Grandpa snored like a steam train so they didn't share a bedroom.)

She remained, until Alzheimer's disease robbed her of her essence, both strong and sweet. She could be feisty—once she chased an un-wanted suitor from her home with a large rock. But she tucked her chin shyly whenever Grandpa kissed her—and they were married for more than 59 years.

Grandma loved to cook and to eat and she passed both enjoyments on to me, teaching me the kitchen basics from the time I was able to see over the top of the counter standing on a stool. Her teenage diaries, written in perfect round script in pencil in ruled school tablets, are full of food references.

March 12, 1911
"Henry (brother), Sophia (niece) and I took walk to the Alaile Valley and we look lunch with us in a basket.... Sophia and I set the table with ferns and a tablecover. We had fried meat, fried eggs and poi and enjoyed it very much."

August 4, 1912
"We had nice food, lots of cake, lots of sandwiches, lots of roasted meats, butter, cheese, deviled ham, beer wine, soda, salad, canned fowl. We had a lot to eat."

September 22, 1912

"Today is Papa's birthday. I made two cakes and Sunday morning at 5, I woke up and lighted the oven, filled three pans with meat and potatoes and one with a chunk of vinha d'ahlos (pickled pork butt), chicken with alecrim (rosemary), too. When the oven was hot, I put it all in. Oh, what a lovely time. We sang lots of songs in English and Portuguese and Hawaiian. In all, the persons were 26 and we enjoyed ourselves."

April 21, 1911

(Having snuck out at night), "Beatrice (niece) and I went and picked mangoes, took the lamp into the dining room, ate mangoes, then potatoes, then bread and jelly, talked all kind of nonsense, danced all kind of ugly way then to bed, our prayers and slept."

June 20, 1912

"First I creamed the butter and sugar, then I beat the whites of 8 eggs, then I put the yolks of the eggs and beat it to cream, and then put 4 cups flour, 1 teaspoon vanilla, 1 cup cornstarch, 1 teaspoon baking powder and 1 cup milk and beat it all up with the cream, then put the whites in and put it in the oven. I made 8 cakes, then had breakfast."

Grandma wanted to be a teacher, but her father insisted she leave school in sixth grade to care for her ailing mother and those of the 10 children who were still at home.

In January 1912, she recorded in her diary, "Marriage is not the only mission for girls in these days of progress." But she did make marriage a mission when she fell in love with Grandpa John Gomes Duarte at the then old-maidish age of 21.

She lived her life in the open, smacking her lips when she enjoyed something, squealing with delight at

Mr. and Mrs. John G. (Ida Sylva) Duarte on their wedding day.

any pleasure, breathing in the scent of fresh laundry or ripe guavas or cooking stew with obvious relish.

In the kitchen, her petite, generously rounded figure moved swiftly and surely on tiny feet. Her hands, so roughened they felt as though coated with plastic, moved confidently among her dishes and bowls, her Revere pots and cast-iron pans, her canning jars and waxed paper freezing cartons.

"Here's how to make things good," she'd say. "You put a pinch of salt in anything sweet, a pinch of sugar in anything not sweet."

"You know how to tell when a cake is done?" she'd ask, wiggling her nose exaggeratedly. "Sniff. Once you smell it, it's almost pau. You gotta watch, but no slam the oven door!"

"Don't be afraid of vinegar," she in-structed. "Vinegar is Portuguese."

"Always plant alecrim (rosemary) outside the kitchen door," she directed. "Keeps away the evil eye."

"Salt is good for you but don't use too much pepper," she said, getting it precisely backward. "Pepper causes heart attacks. You sneeze and you have a heart attack."

I remember watching her dredge beef chunks in seasoned flour. It smelled so good that I begged for a taste. "OK," she said. "But it won't taste like anything." She was right. It didn't. "Gotta cook 'em long time. Long time. Then the flavor come out."

"Wash the rice," she said, every afternoon about 4. Dinner would be on the table at 5. The rice pot was a round, lipped vessel from Japan, with a lid that fit into the lip and danced with a metallic rhythm when the water boiled.

"Everything go hula around me," she said, merrily. She owned a Savage brand washer that did, indeed, hula across the washroom floor when it got going with a big load.

She never sat down to a holiday dinner. She hovered, trotted back and forth to the kitchen, slapped her head and said, "I forgot the olives" every Christmas. The first sign of her Alzheimer's was when she threw out the turkey drippings before we made Thanksgiving gravy a few years before she died. "Mom!" my mother cried. And we both looked at her puzzled face, stricken.

Almost every entry in her girlhood journals begins: *"Woke up, said P., started fire, fed can(aries), cleaned house, when the fire was ready, baked bread."*

She baked in the forno, the brick oven her mason-father had built. At one point, she chronicles the laborious process of clearing the oven of ashes, using a wet "mop" of banana leaves to clean the oven floor, testing the oven temperature with a scattering of flour, sliding the loaves into the oven with the wooden peel.

She was the envy of many of her friends when she became one of the first to be given an electric mixer as an aid to cake-baking. She had dozens of gelatin-based recipes in her penciled notebooks because she adapted early to the 1930s electric ice box revolution. The minute sliced bread and cake mixes and TV dinners came along, she was an early adapter to those, too.

She was in her 70s. Tired perhaps. There's a temptation to romanticize old foodways but she embraced modern shortcuts with fervor. YOU try getting up before dawn to sweep ashes out of a brick oven every day.

Every good thing I am, I owe to my grandmother. Every smart thing I am, I owe to my mother, whom Grandma encouraged to shun early marriage and get an education. Grandma's creased and gentle hands put my feet on the journey that led to becoming not only a writer but a food writer.

Every holiday, my only wish is one that will never be granted: To be with her in her neat, white-painted kitchen with the greenware plates and the soup pot that was built right into the stove, making soup, baking bread, roasting a turkey, learning to make gravy, listening to her stories.

Variações

VARIATIONS ON A PORTUGUESE THEME

For this all-new chapter, we talked with chefs, Neighbor Island folk, travelers to Portugal and a lover of all things Brazilian. Though I recognized the flavors of Portugal in all the dishes they shared, the techniques, the combinations, the subtle influences of cultures from around the world, broadened my horizons, and they will yours, too.

HAWAI'I'S BEST-KNOWN PORTUGUESE CHEF: GEORGE GOMES JR.

George Gomes Jr. was always going to be a chef. From toddler time, he'd hold on to his Great-grandma Alexandrina Soares' apron as she circled her Kalihi kitchen.

Later, he tagged along behind his grandfather, Frank Simon, Jr., who was "the real cook" in the household. Young George would pester Grandpa with questions. "I was the only one who cared or listened at that time," he said. "He is a huge factor in what I do today." His late father, who died just this year, taught him hunting, butchering and smoking.

The kitchen, recalls the 57-year-old chef, was his sanctuary, his safe place.

Born on O'ahu, he moved with his family to a cedar home on a small ranch in Ahualoa on the Hāmākua Coast when he was still a small boy. "Everything was about food; everything centered on the table," he said.

And whatever they ate, they grew or foraged or bartered for as much as possible: pigs, chickens, wild boar, ranch cattle, vegetables and fruits. There was, and still is, a butcher shop on the property and "smoke meat," as well as homemade sausage and fish, were at the center of plates.

"You don't go to the store," he said. "Part of growing up in that culture was not just about cooking, it was about a true farm-to-table lifestyle," he said.

Since the age of 15, he has carried this vision with him to every kitchen in which he's worked, planting herbs and vegetables in hotel gardens, taking his home-smoked meats into restaurants, liaising with local farmers on the Big Island and in stints on Maui, O'ahu and further afield. He has worked hotel chains throughout Hawai'i and is now executive chef at the Royal Kona Resort. And he has guested around the world: Japan, Portugal, Italy and France.

"As chefs, it's really what we should be doing," he said of farm-to-table.

When he muses about the foods of his childhood, the memories flow effortlessly. He tears up.

His mom was bread; his dad was rice and smoked meats; his grandmas were soup. His favorite was the quixotically named "French Stew" of his grandmother, Caroline Simon: tough, old chickens simmered slow and long with pimentos, olives, garlic, onions, bay leaves and fresh homemade refogado (tomato sauce).

Fava bean salad with garlic, onion, vinegar and parsley. Vinha d'ahlos made with wine as well as vinegar and great handfuls of garlic and chilies; they'd strain out the garlic after, fry it and use it as garnish. "We like spice!," he says.

Spinas (fish spine), "aku bone," roasted with sizzling olive oil on top or fried with just a dusting of flour, always with vinegar marinade. Bacalhao (salt cod) salad. He pauses, smiling. "Grandma Adelaide drank a jigger of vinegar every day." Sardines from the can with chili peppers.

Fried potatoes, rice baked in broth. "We (Portuguese) invented rice and potatoes on the same plate," he said. His dad's red bean soup with homemade linguiça sausage. Lima bean soup with potatoes and ham hock. They'd carve the fat off the hock. "We loved the fat," he said. "That was the best part." (I used to drive my grandmother nuts by fishing the hocks out of the soup and carving off the rind, which I would chew with great relish.)

To him, a real home cook or chef considers recipes a rough guideline. "You use your senses, you consider the ingredients you have, their flavor profile. You feel it, you touch it, you smell it, you listen to it cooking, you watch it, and you taste it," he said. If you do this, "you can translate anything from your memory, even if you never got the recipe," he said.

He knows many chefs think of Portuguese food as simple, rustic, unsophisticated.

But, he says, "The simplest food is the very hardest to do because the ingredients have to speak. There is nothing to hide behind."

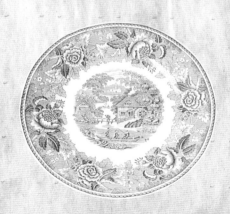

ESCABECHE: WORLD FOOD

One day, chef George Gomes Jr., who had promised to help me with the fresh chapter for this book, posted a photo of escabeche, a marinated fish dish, on Facebook. He had been pondering what dish he would contribute and I immediately posted: "George! I want this dish."

I knew nothing about it. I just knew it was pretty and I loved the word, escabeche (es-kah-besh, or in some forms of Spanish, es-kah-bay-chay). Before I visited him for a tasting at the Royal Kona Resort, I launched into an Internet and cookbook search that told me I had stumbled on a rich culinary vein. In a hundred different versions, this piquant, healthy and quick-to-prepare dish is found wherever Spanish, Portuguese, French and other Europeans have touched the world's cultures.

In Hawai'i, I doubt anyone ever called it by its proper name: Our primitive, no-fuss version goes by the local-boy name "Pickle Fish." Cut fish (or use small, whole ones), dust with flour, fry, douse with vinegary marinade. Serve as pūpū.

Many more sophisticated versions are made around the world but all recipes have this in common: fish, fried, and marinated with vinegar and, often, slivered carrots.

George's version (see page 7) comes from, of all places, Japan, and uses rice vinegar, dashi and wasabi powders and tempura batter.

Then, during a photo session, I asked chef George Mavrothalassitis about escabeche and learned the details of his father's Greek-Provencal recipe: whole, fresh fried sardines (often left over from the previous night's restaurant service), drowned in red wine vinegar and "one ton" of garlic, marinated overnight and served at room temperature as an hors d'oeuvre, or bar food.

Later, I questioned a Filipina elder, a great home cook named Norma Padua, about whether she had heard of escabeche in the Philippines. She looked surprised. "Of course, we make it all the time." Filipino versions feature whole fish (grouper, tilapia), lots of ginger and garlic, onion, shoyu, palm vinegar or even pineapple juice, and a little brown sugar.

Admission: I'm not much of a fish eater; my family lived in the mountains and nobody fished. But I fell in love with every version of escabeche that I tried, and found it one of the easiest recipes ever to master. A thing to know is that the dish only works with oilier fish (a sad experiment with firmer fish yielded very dry, dense nuggets). The technique remains the same the world over: fried fish (floured or battered) and a tart and sometimes spicy, sometimes sweetish marinade; aromatics and vegetables often present, but optional.

Feeding friends in Hilo during a research trip, it made a quick and colorful entrée that everyone enjoyed—my local hosts and a charming couple from India, where escabeche is made by the Portuguese-influenced regions of Goa and environs along the west coast.

As we say in my house, "THIS one goes in the cookbook!"

GEORGE GOMES'
ASIAN ESCABECHE
Makes 2 pūpū servings

Georg Gomes Jr. encountered this seafood tempura dish while guest-chefing in Japan. It's a version of the marinated fish dish called escabeche, known wherever Spanish or Portuguese touched down in their voyages of exploration and colonization, and in French Provencal cuisine. This version makes two appetizer-size servings but the recipe is flexible; make as much as you like.

On the day he made the dish for me in his kitchen at the Royal Kona Resort, Gomes used kalikali, a juvenile opakapaka.

George makes his own tempura batter from rice flour, all-purpose flour, wasabi powder, salt and ice water. I use a mix and it's still delish. Add ½ teaspoon teaspoon wasabi powder to the mix for a little more kick.

George likes to add a couple of fresh bay leaves; you can find fresh bay at some farmer's markets. If you only have access to hard, dried bay leaves, skip this ingredient.

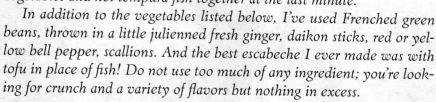

Finally, George likes pica (hot!); I have a more timid tongue. I recommend starting with one ni'oi (small, hot, red Hawaiian chili) and adding a second only if the sauce isn't spicy enough for you.

I've arranged this recipe in chef-like fashion, as George did, with all ingredients prepped in individual bowls; throw the stir-fried vegetables and hot tempura fish together at the last minute.

In addition to the vegetables listed below, I've used Frenched green beans, thrown in a little julienned fresh ginger, daikon sticks, red or yellow bell pepper, scallions. And the best escabeche I ever made was with tofu in place of fish! Do not use too much of any ingredient; you're looking for crunch and a variety of flavors but nothing in excess.

(continued on the next page)

Variations on a Portuguese Theme

6 ounces fresh, boneless, slightly oily, white-fleshed fillets of
  fish (opakapaka, onaga, opah, mahimahi, monchong, cod
  or butterfish)
Sea salt and freshly ground pepper
One recipe tempura batter
2 tablespoons thinly sliced fresh garlic
½ shallot, thinly sliced
1 small carrot, julienned (cut into sticks)
2 fresh bay leaves (do not used dried)
1 teaspoon Thai fried garlic (optional)
1 teaspoon dashi powder
3 tablespoons rice vinegar
1 to 2 small niʻoi (small, hot,
  Hawaiian red peppers),
  minced
Pinch sugar
Pinch salt
2 tablespoons olive oil
Two sprigs leafy celery ends
5 to 6 ripe cherry tomatoes, halved
1 tablespoon minced flat-leaf parsley

Cut fish into 1 by 1½-inch rectangles. Sprinkle with salt and pepper. In
a bowl, prepare tempura batter. Set aside.

Prep the garlic, shallots and carrots (and other vegetables, as desired) as
directed and place in individual bowls. Set aside.

In a bowl, combine dashi powder, rice vinegar, minced niʻoi,
sugar and salt. Set aside.

In a sauté pan, heat olive oil
gently over medium heat. Heat
garlic and shallots just until
limp and translucent; do not
brown. Add carrots, bay leaves

Variações

and fried garlic and heat until warmed. Remove from heat, place pan on cutting board and add dashi-vinegar mixture, stirring and allowing to cook in residual heat. Taste and correct seasonings.

Heat 2 inches of vegetable oil in wok or frying pan to 365°F. Drag fish pieces through batter and drain excess. Deep-fry battered fish until golden. Place in pan with vegetables and sauce, spoon sauce over fish. Taste and correct seasonings. Place tempura-vegetable mixture on warmed serving plates. Garnish with celery ends, cherry tomatoes and parsley. Serve immediately.

CONQUERING THE WORLD:
CHEF GEORGE MAVROTHALASSITIS
WITH PASTRY CHEF BEVERLY LUK

On a summer trip to his French homeland, uber-chef George Mavrothalassitis, whose Chef Mavro Restaurant in Honolulu has earned the AAA Five Diamond Award for 11 years consecutively, and his business-partner wife, Donna Jung, decided to tuck in a short trip to the Portuguese capitol of Lisboa (Lisbon).

Both were surprised by how much they liked it. They relished the rustic food, the historic buildings, the welcoming people, and the low prices.

Most of all, they fell in love with a specialty of the region, Pasteis de Belem, custard tarts encased in little fluted beds of puff pastry. Belem is a historic neighborhood in Lisbon where the riotously hectic Café Belem serves thousands of these pastries every day.

"We ate them every day," Jung said of the pastries. At Café Belem, they're sold in cleverly built tall, hexagonal boxes. They tried the pasteis elsewhere, but the Café is the epicenter (https://pasteisdebelem.pt/en/).

"It's crazy," said "Mavro", "A million people, Japanese tourists taking selfies. A ton of local people, too. You have to fight your way through the line. We ate the pastries in the taxi. I had no expectations and when I bite inside, I was like, 'Oh, my God!'" So light, so crispy so beautiful," he said.

"We only spent two days but we packed a lot into it," said Jung. They ate at Belcanto, the two Michelin star restaurant of Jose Avillez. "He's a god in Portugal," said Mavro. "To have two Michelin in Portugal right around the corner from our hotel, I couldn't believe it."

"The food is cheap!" Mavro ex-

claimed. "Two Michelin-star, $17 a person. Huge lobster, $100 the whole meal. It's crayzeee!" (Mavro invariably speaks of food in exclamation marks.)

The food is very simple but very surprising. No sauces, bake-steam-grill but the fish is fresh and the Portuguese version of brandade (a cream and salt cod gratin very popular in his native Marseilles) earned his own two stars.

When he told his young but extremely skilled pastry chef, Beverly Luk, about the pasteis, she knew just what he meant. She recalled the Portuguese-influenced pastry of Macau, a seaside city in her native Hong Kong. "it's a very sweet custard but very well balanced and buttery pastry," she said. "It's very similar to a Chinese custard tart," a favorite in Hawai'i.

When I asked George and Donna to help with this book, they thought of Pasteis de Belem immediately. But there was a little hiccup. Attempting not to make work for the perennially busy chef, I suggested using frozen commercial puff pastry. Donna's answer burned through the Internet. She said George would rather not start if he wasn't going to work from scratch. (Ooops, sorry!)

So he and Luk conspired on hand-made puff pastry (sheets of dough spread with cold butter and folded, folded, folded to create a crisp explosion in the mouth at the first bite). They made six-layer pattons (blocks), shaped them jelly roll style, wrapped them carefully and refrigerated them. For our photo shoot, they defrosted the dough, cut the rolls about an inch apart and pressed the pieces into fluted forms before baking.

"The food culture to me is always person to person. It's like a dough; you need to touch it," Mavro said.

I touched my sample with its characteristic tracery of browned spots on top for about two minutes and then ... sybaritically gone!

Pasteis de Belem
CUSTARD IN PUFF PASTRY SHELLS
Makes 18 pastries

Pasteis de Belem is a quintessential Portuguese doce (sweets): Eggs, eggs, eggs, sugar, sugar, sugar.

I loaned Chef George Mavrothassitis and his pastry chef, Beverly Luk, a home cooking version of the famed Lisbon specialty and it met their approval. I've given the standard cup measures along with the weights here, because the latter is the gold standard for pastry, a science as much as an art. Weigh instead of measure for best results.

The tricky point here is the baking. Know your oven; test it, and if it runs hot, reduce the temperature or the cooking time. Watch these carefully, checking after 15, 20, 25 minutes.

And, though Mavro will kill me when he reads this, if you haven't mastered puff pastry, use frozen puff pastry shells and make the custard from scratch. The custard can be made in advance and refrigerated in an airtight container.

To learn about puff pastry, check Julia Child's recipe in "Mastering the Art of French Cooking" by Child with Louisette Bertholle and Simone Beck, or do a Google search for Julia Child and Michel Richard's video on puff pastry technique). The process is time-consuming but far superior to any frozen product.

Custard in puff pastry shells
2 cups granulated sugar (500 ml)
³/₄ cup water (175 ml)
¼ cup all-purpose flour (50 ml)
2 cups cold milk (500 ml)
2 teaspoons finely grated lemon zest (10 ml)
8 egg yolks
1 pound puff pastry (500 g)
Ground cinnamon (optional)

(recipe continued on page 14)

Variações

In a saucepan, combine sugar and water. Boil over medium heat for 10-12 minutes, or until sugars thread off the end of a spoon. Set aside and allow to cool.

In a small saucepan, blend flour and ¼ cup (50 ml) cold milk. Gradually whisk and stir in 1¾ cups (425 ml) milk and lemon rind. Bring to a boil over medium heat, stirring continually, until mixtures comes to a boil. Continue cooking, stirring, for 2 to 3 minutes, until thickened. Remove from heat and set aside to cool.

In a large bowl, whisk together egg yolks. Gradually pour a thin spread of sugar syrup into yolks, followed by cooled milk mixture. Blend well; strain and set custard aside.

Preheat oven to 450°F. Adjust racks so that tarts may be baked in center of the oven.

On a lightly floured surface, roll out half the puff pastry into a 12-inch square about ⅜-inch thick. Cut out nine 4-inch circles. With damp fingers, fit into muffin tins or tart molds. If pastry begins to soften, chill 30 minutes and resume rolling and/or shaping.

Fill tart shells half-full with custard filling. Bake tarts (as below), then repeat with remaining pastry dough. NOTE: Each half-batch of nine is done separately because the tarts must be baked in a single batch in the oven; two batches at a time won't cook evenly.

Set oven rack to second-highest position. Bake shells in preheated 450-degree oven for 30 minutes or until pastry is partially caramelized (spotted or striated with browned bits).

If using cinnamon, sprinkle tarts with a few drops of cold water and scatter lightly with cinnamon. Cool 5 minutes. Run a knife around edges of muffin tins and carefully remove tarts to a wire rack (bottoms will cool as custard sets). Roll out remaining dough and prepare the next nine tarts.

BRAZIL: THE "OTHER" PORTUGAL: SANDY TSUKIYAMA

Radio show host, translator, singer and ethnomusicologist Sandy Tsukiyama is a puzzlement to many. How does an ethnically Japanese local girl come to speak fluent Portuguese (both the Brazilian and Mainland Portuguese forms), steeped in the food, culture, history and the music of Brazil?

Two answers:

- A Japanese diaspora in the late 19th century that mirrors that of the Portuguese Atlantic Islanders who emigrated to Hawai'i.

- And love, bossa nova love. That darned "Girl from Ipanema."

Tsukiyama always knew she had relatives in Brazil on her mother's side, but her father's family had chosen Hawai'i. (Her parents met on a return trip to Japan.) Like the Portuguese, Japanese were seafarers who settled in small pockets around the world.

When difficult economic and social times hit Japan during the feaudal Meiji period, other governments, including Hawai'i, sent emisseries to the country to recruit workers, just as Dr. William Hillebrand drafted workers in the Portuguese Atlantic Islands. The Japanese and Portuguese began their treks abroad at about the same time, in the 1880s.

Today, the home of Carnival and samba is also home to the largest number of Japanese citizens outside the homeland, more than 1.5 million people.

So, not to strange one Manoa girl with roots on Shikoku and Kyushu Islands, found her way to Brazil.

But about that other girl, the one from Ipanema.

"I first heard that song when I was 9 years old," recalled Tsukiyama. It was a life-altering moment. "I was asking, 'What is this? What kind of strange accent is that? Where is Ipanama, some kind of mythical place?'"

The fire was lit. Tsukiyama graduated from Roosevelt High School and UH Manoa, studied Spanish and Portuguese and began traveling to Brazil where she met her extended family. She eventually received a fellowship from the Universidade Federal do Rio de Janeiro Escola de Música, studying Western African influences on music in the Americas. She reveled in such events as the century-old Japanese Fest in Sao Paulo.

Along the way, Tsukiyama married musician Carlinhos "Pandeiro de Auro" ("Golden Tamborine") de Oliveira, a master of the Brazilian tuneable tamborine. They divided their time between Brazil and Hawai'i until they parted, though remaining friends and proponents of Brazilian regional musics and instruments, and Sandy returned to the Islands in 1983.

I first met her in the early '90s when I was studying "Portuguese For Foreigners" with the late Dona Cecy Browne (who despaired of me because I had studied Spanish and kept speaking "Spanuguese" in class). Browne hosted a class-ending feast each session and Sandy, an enthusiastic home cook who raises rabbits for meat, knows how to find the best food prices for everything, and keeps a garden, brought feijoada, the national dish of Brazil, a rich bean stew. I loved it, but we lost touch although I often listen to Tsukiyama's Hawaii Public Radio show, "The Brazilian Experience" (Sundays, 6 to 8 PM, HPR-1).

When I began wondering who to work with on this new chapter, Tsukiyama came to mind and, although she left the time-consuming feijoada to me, serving as my chief tester and advisor, she spent a morning in my kitchen preparing a much simpler dish that stole my cheese-loving heart: Pao de Queijo (cheese bread). These delicious bites of cassava flour, milk, egg and cheese are a staple at Hawaii Public Radio events, where they disappear faster than matching funds during a pledge drive. Knowledgeable, witty, funny and down-to-earth, Tsukiyama made my day with her company, this dish and an end to the puzzlement about the Japanese Brazilian.

Pão de Queijo
BRAZILIAN CHEESE PUFFS
Makes 6 pūpū servings

D o not be afraid of the term "bread"; these rich, quick-to-make pupu puffs are within the range of a kitchen-savvy child. Says Sandy Tsukiyama: "Everyone loves them. Everyone asks for the recipe. When I go to Brazilian parties, people are lined up in front of the stove. You just throw 'em in a basket and they're gone."

Two difficulties present themselves but are easily remedied.

- The main ingredient, cassava starch (manioc, yuca or tapioca flour), polvilho azedo in Brazilian Portuguese, takes some finding. On O'ahu, Mercado de la Raza stocks it. Or find it online. This is a sour, acidic version; do not use povilho aduce, the sweet type.

- Achieving the right texture is key: too dry and the dough will crumble, too wet and the breadlets will be tough. You're looking for smooth and a little wet.

Other than that, the only thing to decide is what cheese to use. Sandy, being a thrifty sort, uses dry grated Parmesan, the stuff in the green can (no kidding, and I said I'd never let it pass my doorstep). The Brazilian staple for this dish, quiejo minas meia cura, is unavailable here except online. Pao de queijo-deprived Brazilian expatriates have learned to use fresh-grated Parmesan, or half and half Parmesan and mozzarella, or sometimes Mexican cheeses.

Unbaked pao de quiejo dough can be frozen, well-wrapped, for about a month, then defrosted in the refrigerator and baked. And they're gluten-free.

2 cups cassava starch (povilho azedo)
2 cups Kraft grated Parmesan (the infamous green can)
1 cup milk, scalded
¹/₃ to ¹/₂ cup vegetable oil
1 egg, lightly beaten

(continued on the next page)

Preheat oven to 350°F. Line a baking sheet with aluminum foil or kitchen parchment.

In a medium bowl, combine starch and cheese, forming a well in the center. Scald milk (heat over medium-high until bubbles form around the edge). Pour scalded milk and oil into starch-cheese mixture and, with kitchen-gloved hands, mix to combine. Add egg. If the mixture is too dry add a second egg or some hot water. Pinch off sufficient dough to make a golfball-size round, rolling between your palms. Space rounds an inch apart on baking sheet.

Bake at 350°F for 12 to 15 minutes, until golden brown and puffy.

Note: Some recipes call for a larger proportion of liquid to starch and cheese, resulting in a soft, lumpy batter that's incorporated in a blender or food processor, then dropped by tablespoonsfull onto the baking sheet.

Variações

HAWAI'I STYLE: BOBBY CAMARA

Bobby Camara is a man of his words. Plural.

Retired from a 30-year-career with Volcanoes National Park, he lives in the rainforest, has firm opinions on everything and relishes delivering a to-the-point lectures on his views.

Malassadas, for example: not too big, no frou-frou fillings, no cinnamon sugar, no vanilla. instead, his Gramma Matilda Rapozo's "secret ingredient"—lemon extract. Once you taste these airy, cakey pastries, unlike any I've ever had before, and still delicious when they're cold (!!!), you have to conclude he knows of what he speaks.

When he shares recipes, he laces the measurements and instructions with the valuable-as-gold tips that so help a novice.

His world-changing sheet-pan vinha d'ahlos (pickled meat), is another example. So easy, no frying. After a glorious, rain-drenched day talking story and cooking at his compact cottage full of artwork and mementos, I lived on leftover vinha d'ahlos for three days. Tip: Cut the meat into large chunks (2-by-3 inches or more) as it will shrink into nasty little dry nuggets otherwise.

Camara, 67, grew up in the Honoka'a near his Gramma Rapozo's Pa'auhau home, in an extended family whose names were Camara, Carvalho, Rapozo and Castro. They were a self-sufficient family, keeping a huge garden, tending animals, bartering with others. His father, a sugar plantation mechanic, leased a gulch where he kept a few cattle. "We had oxtail stew once a year, 'cause a cow only get one tail," Camara said, recalling days when treats were rare and much appreciated.

Pa'auhau was composed of ethnically diverse camps. Although he is pure Portuguese, Camara never defined himself by his ethnicity. He prefers to be called "local." Interacting with neighbors, attending their community celebrations, he learned to love Korean meat jun, Puerto Rican gandule rice, Japanese cone sushi (inari), Hawaiian laulau and these were on the table along with Portuguese soups, pickled meats, fresh garden vegetables sautéed in olive oil and garlic

"If you went to somebody's house to eat and had something ʻono, you say, 'How do you do this?' And they'd say, "Come. I show you.,'" said Camara.

"Nothing was fancy," he said. When I mentioned using bay leaf, he almost snorted; "We didn't have that. People grew what they considered basic." (Although, Bobby, bay leaf grows here prolifically.)

The stores of Hilo were a two-hour drive away then; trips to buy staples were well-spaced. "We ate what we had. There was no fast food. We couldn't afford to go to restaurants, even if there were any. We were poor. Your radius of living was very, very small (but) nobody was bored. Everybody had fun."

Life revolved around their Catholic church, Our Lady of Lourdes. He recalls the annual feast when parishioners would band together to make 10,000 laulau. Ranchers contributed beef; pig farmers sent pork; fishermen their catch. The church acquired an immense (6- by 10-foot) pot once used to boil cane juice in which the laulau would steam.

Bobby went to Oregon State University for two years, then transferred to UH-Mānoa, where rented a house with friends. That's when he learned to replicate the foods of his childhood. "We had no money... You wanna eat, you gotta cook. So you make rice and go out and see what you can find," he said. After he returned to Hawaiʻi Island in 1974, he smartly teased out his relatives' best recipes.

A great friend of the late food historian Nan Piʻianaia, who introduced Camara to me during the organization of Slow Food here, Camara has a natural inclination to think of things historically and culturally.

In an early conversation for this book, he made a point worth noting: Portuguese recipes on the Internet, by and large, come from East Coast Mainland communities, or mainland Portugal. "They are not the way we cook," he said. "Our ʻPortuguese' cooking is unique to this ʻaina, based on making do with what you had to achieve the flavors that you loved."

GRAMMA RAPOZO'S MALASSADAS
Makes about 24 malassadas

Bobby Camara's wide circle of friends come running when he makes Gramma Rapozo's Malassadas. They are, indeed, unique.

Gramma's malassadas-making technique, and Bobby's way with it, are charming. Bobby says he still crosses himself and worries about killing the yeast. "After years of making it, it's still an anxiety," he says. (Bobby, compadre, just "proof" the yeast first; see below). The little round golf ball-size bites do this thing that had me belly laughing: If they're correctly shaped, they fry on one side and then turn themselves over like the magic tea service that washes itself in Merlin's wizard cottage.

Deep-fat frying is a skill that takes some learning, but is not as complicated or difficult as the length of the cooking instructions makes it seem. Most important: rigorous temperature control, and using your senses (and a little nibble-testing here and there) to judge proper doneness.

Bobby Camara's malassada tips (and Wanda's, too):

- Set up a work area on a counter or table adjacent to the cooking. Line workspace with brown paper bags split to open flat upon which to drain the fresh malassadas. (Do not use newspaper with its toxic inks.)

- Bobby uses a restaurant-size, 10-quart, stainless steel mixing bowl to accommodate multiple batches.

- For temperature-stable oil, Bobby uses an old-timey appliance he inherited from his mother: a countertop skillet with a thermostat that accurately maintains the set temperature. (Try thrift stores or online.) A heavy-bottomed Dutch oven, skillet or wok is fine. But if you use the stovetop, a

(continued on the next page)

frying thermometer (150- to 400-degree Fahrenheit range) is a must. Oil temperature steady at 365°F is vital to prevent gooey centers or overdone exteriors.

- If you use bulk yeast, ¼ ounce (7 grams or 2 rounded teaspoonsfull) are equivalents for one package yeast. Bobby uses Fleischman's envelopes; Wanda buys SAF brand in bulk.

- Bobby rightly recommends top-quality vegetable oil (he likes Wesson); cheap vegetable oils break down in deep frying, creating off flavors.

- Start with ½ teaspoon lemon extract; use more on subsequent batches if you prefer.

- While Bobby generally makes a quadruple batch, start with the single batch here to get the feel of the batter, cooking time, texture and flavor.

- Bobby uses a sharp-edged old silver tablespoon to measure the batter; the edge removes overflow that causes misshapen, undercooked donuts. For compact, puffy rounds, note his scooping technique in the text of the recipe.

- Start with a single "tester" ball of dough; drop in 365-degree Fahrenheit oil; fry to brown on one side; the little round should turn itself, if it doesn't, turn with chopsticks. Chopsticks are delicate; tongs manhandle the donuts.

1 cup whole milk
1 package yeast (2 rounded teaspoonsfull)
3 cups all-purpose flour
½ teaspoon salt
½ cup white sugar
4 eggs
½ to 1 teaspoon lemon extract
Vegetable oil for frying

In a small saucepan, scald milk (heat on medium-high until small bubbles form around the edge of the pot); immediately remove from heat. Cool to lukewarm, 100 to 110°F (or dribble a few drops on your wrist; if it warm but not burning, it's safe). Add yeast and stir with fork or mini-whisk to break up any lumps; "proof" by waiting two minutes to see if it bubbles and foams gently.

Place the flour, salt and sugar in a large mixing bowl. Make a well in the center; stir to combine. In a medium mixing bowl, beat eggs until well-blended but not foamy. Add lemon extract. Stir milk-yeast mixture into egg mixture. Pour wet mixture into well in flour mixture and stir with a wooden spoon until incorporated. The batter will be rough, wet and sticky, somewhere between cake batter and soft bread dough.

Cover bowl with a dish towel and place in a warm, draft-free place to rise for two hours.

Pour oil into countertop frying pan or heavy-bottomed Dutch oven or deep cast-iron frying pan to the depth of 2 inches. Heat to 365°F; check temperature frequently. Donuts absorb heat and lower the temperature so it may need adjustment, or a pause between batches.

When the oil reaches temperature, use a tablespoon (not a measuring spoon, regular tableware) to gather up a tablespoon-sized clump of batter, scraping against the side of the bowl to remove excess and cut off any "strings." Slide the batter into the oil by running your thumb down the bowl of the spoon. You're looking for a near-perfect round.

Start with one "tester." Fry until brown on bottom; it should turn itself, but if it doesn't turn with chopsticks to cook both sides evenly. The donut will emerge about 2½ inches in diameter, nearly spherical but sometimes with odd bumps and lumps and quite browned. Remove to drain on paper bags. Roll in sugar, if desired. Split the malassada to be sure it's fully cooked; it will appear cakey and bubbly inside, not gooey or smooth. Check temperature and adjust as needed.

Continue with remaining dough, carefully monitoring temperature, which will fall during cooking.

Vinha d'Ahlos Meat Camara

Makes 6 to 8 servings

Bobby Camara's is by far the easiest and most streamlined technique I've ever found and I doubt I'll follow my Grandma's approach (marinate, roast, slice, fry, to make "tresmoses," browned nuggets of pork). His family's technique: Marinate thick chunks of meat in vinegar, water, garlic, Hawaiian peppers and Hawaiian salt; simmer briefly with halved new potatoes; drain and roast in sheet pan with halved new potatoes. Done.

One interesting note: Without exception, people familiar with old-time vinha d'ahlos say that, in the day, the meat was marinated at room temperature for two or three days; not the 24 hours usually recommended today.

Even if your family made different choices (wine as well as vinegar, more or fewer peppers and cloves of garlic, pickling spice or Portuguese 5-Spice), this technique eliminates a lot of fuss. Here's a free-form recipe.

Large (3- by 3-inch) chunks chuck roast and pork butt, enough to fill one rimmed baking sheet
2 parts vinegar
1 part water
1 head garlic, peeled and smashed
7 niʻoi (small hot red Hawaiian peppers)
Handful of Hawaiian salt
1 to 2 pounds skin-on red potatoes, halved

In a non-reactive bowl, marinate meats in vinegar and water with garlic, peppers and salt two days at room temperature (cover with kitchen towel, not plastic wrap; smelling the marinade is part of the appetite-building experience). Stir a couple of times a day.

Place meats and marinade in a large soup pot with potatoes, bring to a boil, skim foam and reduce heat. Simmer gently 20 minutes, no longer, or meat will fall apart. Drain.

Spread ingredients on an oiled sheet pan and roast at 350°F for 45 minutes. Check at 35 minutes; the pieces should be moist inside, crisped and browned outside. Serve hot or at room temperature.

WHAT I LEARNED: WANDA ADAMS

I n 2014, when *A Portuguese Kitchen* was first released, I thought I was done. The recipes weren't. They kept coming. Here are a few I've learned in the past five years.

LEMON "VINHA D'AHLOS" PORK ROAST WITH SALSA LIMÃO E MANTEIGA

Makes 4 to 6 servings
For fewer servings, see the note at the end

C ontinuing with the theme of up-dating classic Portuguese recipes, I've always wanted to make vinha d'ahlos (pickled meats) with lemon juice instead of the usual vinegar. Then I got the idea of serving it in a light beaurre blanc (white butter sauce).

For this, you can marinate and roast a pork butt roast (the least expensive op-tion), but you can, instead, marinate and pan-fry pork chops, boneless pork cutlets, even flattened chicken breast or turkey breast.

I first ran across lemon butter sauce in Mary Sue Milliken and Susan Feniger's "City Cuisine" (1989). I am not a trained culinarian so had little understanding of sauces. I never could master beurre blanc until I realized that an electric stove (which most home cooks use) allows little heat control. And the secret of successful, creamy textured beaurre blanc is cold butter in warm (not hot) broth.

So I made the broth first, simmered the sauce to reduce by half and let it cool to lukewarm, then swirled in the chilled butter pieces. Mirac-ulous! My husband voted this in the top ten of all time. The greens add *a needed contrast. Other accompaniments: hot rice, crusty fresh bread, thin-sliced fried potatoes.*

For the roast and marinade:
2 pounds pork butt roast
Juice and zest of 2 lemons
4 to 6 cloves garlic, minced
1½ tablespoons Hawaiian salt or flaked salt
Drizzle of piripiri (Portuguese chili condiment; see page 36)
   OR chili peppah wattah OR ½ to 1 Hawaiian chili, finely chopped
Several cranks of fresh-ground pepper
¼ cup minced flat-leaf parsley

For the sauce:
¾ large white onion or sweet onion, minced (or 10 shallots)
2 tablespoons minced flat-leaf parsley
⅔ cup lemon juice
⅔ cup chicken stock or desired broth, leftover gravy, drippings from roasting
⅔ cup dry white wine
6 tablespoons chilled butter, cut into slices
Salt and pepper to taste

For the greens:
3 cups julienned Portuguese cabbage
   OR baby kale and baby spinach
Water
1 tablespoon butter

Trim the surface fat from the pork butt , cut fat into strips and render in a saute pan over medium-high heat; reduce heat if fat begins to scorch. Once pieces are crisp and golden, remove and discard.* Brown the roast in the fat on all sides. Remove from heat, drain and retain drippings for further use in this recipe.

While roast is cooling enough to touch, combine lemon juice and zest, salt, piripiri, pepper and parsley in a bowl or zippered plastic bag, stirring and massaging to make a paste. Place the roast in this marinade, turn to coat and allow to season 4 hours or longer, up to overnight, turning periodically. Bring to room temperature before roasting.

Pre-heat oven to 375°F and roast pork to 145°F internal temperature, about 45 minutes.

Meanwhile, sweat onions or shallots with remaining drippings over medium-low heat. Do not allow to brown; they should be limp and translucent. Add lemon juice, chicken stock and wine, bring to a boil, then gently simmer to reduce by half (20 to 30 minutes). Reduce heat to very low and hold.

To prepare greens, wash and leave water clinging to leaves. Place in a preheated medium-high saute pan or wok and throw in remaining tablespoon of butter. Stir until wilted. Keep warm.

When the roast is done, tent with heavy-duty foil on a cutting board and allow to rest 10 to 15 minutes before carving into slices.

Meanwhile, begin to swirl butter, one piece at a time, into reduced lemon-broth-wine mixture. Keep the heat on low; any higher and the sauce will "break," the butter melting too fast and forming a greasy goo. The sauce should be silky and very slightly thickened.

To present, place a bed of greens on a plate, arrange a slice or two of pork roast on the greens and drizzle with sauce.

*Note: For fewer servings, reserve some sauce and greens with meat for another meal. Or salt and eat the cracklings or use as garnish, but that would be sinful. If you don't want to use drippings, use olive oil or butter and discard fat.

Minha Feijoada
MY BRAZIIAN BEAN STEW
(AS GUIDED BY BRAZILIAN-AT-HEART SANDY TSUKIYAMA)
Makes 6 to 8 servings
(depending on how many hungry Brazilians you're serving)

When I was growing up, the only Brazilians we knew were my Grandpa's relatives in Rio de Janeiro (a wealthy merchant who, every day at lunch when the family visited, ate until he fell asleep, shocking my 18-year-old mother).

Today, scratch a North Shore surfer, you'll find a Brazilian. Brazilian music, dance, and martial arts (capoeira) all are popular here.

Feijoada, the national dish of Brazil, looks difficult and time-consuming with its lengthy ingredient list. But it requires the same time investment and kitchen skill as beef stew or Portuguese soup. An overnight soaking for beans, an hour of prep next day, a few hours of unsupervised simmering time (2 to 6, depending on cooking method), a little prep of accompaniments at the end.

The fragrance as the flavors develop and intensify makes the house, as the old song says, a "uma casa Portugueza com certeza," ("truly a Portuguese home").

Feijoada, like most slow-simmered foods, improves with age. Make it a few days in advance, refrigerate and reheat. It freezes well, too.

This folksy dish is like so many of its cousins: What tastes right to you is the feijoada your family served. Without that background, go with your taste preferences.

My first efforts didn't meet the approval of my coach, Hawaii Public Radio "Brazilian Experience" host Sandy Tsukiyama: the meat-to-bean ratio was off, the mixture too dense and chewy. I had become confused by Internet recipes that listed every possible meat you could use, from pork butt to pig feet, smoked meat to sausage.

(continued on the next page)

So I cut it back to essentials: ham hock for broth, bacon, pork butt, jerky or pipikaula, linguiça sausage—and not too much of any of these. Sandy also insisted on the use of green bell pepper and she was right; you don't taste it but it adds something elusive. She is an advocate of the pressure cooker. I use a slow cooker but a heavy Dutch oven is fine, too.

The feijoada experience relies on traditional accompaniments to balance taste and texture: fresh orange slices for acid and crisp bacon-sauteed manioc flour for crunch, rice as an extender and sautéed Portuguese cabbage or collards for garlicky crunch.

1 pound dried black beans
2 slices thick-cut bacon, 2-inch slices
2 ounces pipikaula, chopped, OR naturally flavored beef jerky, soaked in warm water, drained, cut into small pieces
1 large onion, chopped
1 large green bell pepper, seeded, chopped
½ pound linguiça sausage, sliced, quartered
1 pound well-marbled pork butt, bite-size chunks
1 ham hock
3 bay leaves
6 crushed cloves garlic
Salt and pepper
Piri piri (Portuguese chili sauce; see page 40) or hot sauce (optional)
Serving accompaniments: baked long-grain garlic rice (see page 133), orange slices, farofa*, lime and tomato vinaigrette, piripiri or other hot sauce, Portuguese cabbage sautéed in olive oil with garlic (see page 151)

The night before: Place beans in soup pot with water to cover. Bring to a boil, cover, turn off heat and soak overnight.

Cooking day: In a large, deep frying pan or Dutch oven over medium heat, gently cook bacon with pipikaula or jerky to render fat; do not allow bacon to crisp. (If using jerky, retain soaking liquid for later use.) Remove meats and drain on paper towels; place in Dutch oven, slow cooker or pressure cooker. Discard all but 1 tablespoon fat from frying pan. Over medium-low heat, saute onion and bell pepper in fat until limp. Remove vegetables to Dutch oven, slow cooker or pressure cooker. Add pork butt and sausage to remaining fat in frying pan. Brown lightly. Add ham hock, bay leaves, garlic and jerky soaking liquid (if using), ito meats, onions and bell pepper in Dutch oven, slow cooker or pressure cooker. Add water or beef stock to cover (up to 4 cups). Simmer over medium-low heat (consult slow cooker or pressure cooker instructions for desired settings, length of time, amount of liquid) until meats are tender and falling off any bones.

Remove ham hock and any bones or cartilage. Taste and add salt and pepper if desired.

Drain soaked beans; add to meat mixture. Continue to simmer slowly until beans are tender. Taste and correct seasonings with salt and pepper and a few drops piri piri or hot sauce, if desired. If a thicker gravy is desired, remove ½ cup or so of beans, mash well and return to stew.

Serve with traditional accompaniments (above).

* Farofa is the Brazilian answer to buttered bread crumbs; dried manioc flour toasted in fat (bacon or other drippings), it's used as a crunchy-crumbly foil to the rich stew. Manioc flour can be found online or on O'ahu at El Mercado de la Raza.

Bottarga
PORTUGUESE FISHERMEN'S STEW

Makes 4 generous entrée servings;
6 servings as part of a multi-course meal

This recipe of my devising is based on traditional Bacalhau Stew (dried salt cod in chunky tomato sauce). Bacalhau has grown expensive, and it is an acquired taste. I wanted to create a version of this stovetop braise for those who don't care for the main ingredient! The allure of the stew is the salty fish against the sweet, garlickey sauce so I gave fresh Island fish a short sugar-salt cure.

My model for this is an opulent Sicilian dish called bottarga, most often made with rare and costly bluefin tuna but amenable to any moist, oily or slightly oil fish. Fresh black cod (butterfish or sablefish) is perfect but hard to find in Hawai'i, where that species is almost exclusively sold in a misoyaki (miso) marinade; ask at a fish shop if they can reserve some fresh cod for you. Note that the initial curing takes 3 to 4 hours; after that, the fish can be stored up to 24 hours, well-wrapped, in the refrigerator.

¼ **cup coarse kosher salt**
¼ **cup granulated sugar**
⅓ **bunch or more flat-leaf parsley, finely minced (divided use)**
Juice and zest of 1 large lemon
1 pound boneless fish fillets, such as cod, monchong, opah, snapper, mahi, 'ahi, salmon
For the refogado (tomato base): 2 large thinly sliced onions broken into crescents, ⅓ cup fruity olive oil, 6 cloves peeled and chopped garlic, 12 peeled and seeded tomatoes; additional fresh or canned tomatoes as needed
1 cup clam juice, fish stock, dashi or white wine; more as needed*
1 lemon, quartered and seeded

In a small bowl or measuring cup, toss together salt and sugar; stir in minced parsley, reserving a tablespoon or so for garnish; add lemon juice and zest. Gently rinse the fish fillets in cold water, pat dry, slice into pieces about 1½ ounces each, 10 to 12 pieces total.

Variações

In a flat glass baking dish, spread out half the curing mixture, arrange fish on top and sprinkle remaining curing mixture over fish, spreading with spatula to evenly coat. Cover with plastic wrap and cure 3 to 4 hours at room temperature (liquid will be released). Drain off liquid, wipe with paper towel; cover and refrigerate until refogado is ready (overnight is okay).

In a very large saute pan, a Dutch oven or other wide, heavy pan, make refogado with onions, olive oil, garlic and tomatoes. (see page 70 for technique.)

Once the tomato base is a bit jammy and thick; divide in half, reserving one-half for future use (refrigerated or frozen in airtight container). Thin the chunky base to a salsa-type texture with clam juice, fish stock, dashi or dry white wine. Bring to a simmer over medium heat. Arrange fish atop sauce, cover, and simmer gently 7 to 10 minutes, until fish is cooked through.

Serve hot over rice or mihlo (cornmeal porridge, see page 133), garnished generously with minced parsley; pass lemon wedges to squeeze over fish.

Clam juice is my preference but, as with so many old-fashioned ingredients, it can be hard to find. Fish stock has to be made from scratch. But then I remembered powdered dashi packets. Use half a packet with 1 cup boiling water; add more dashi if it needs flavor. And if you don't like any of those options, there's always wine!

Variation: Make the dish cioppino-style by adding pieces of cleaned and shelled shellfish or whole, tiny young squid 3 to 5 minutes after the fillet pieces are added.

Accompaniments: crostini (garlickey toast rounds from baguette), oven-baked long-grain rice, crusty fresh bread or thin-sliced potatoes fried in olive oil.

Pão de Ló Manteiga
GRANDMA SYLVA'S CAKE (BUTTER SPONGE CAKE PORTUGUESE)
Serves 8 or more

In her precious teenaged diaries, my grandmother recorded many meals and cooking experiences (see page xxi). On June 20, 1912, she told of making a cake, Pão de Ló Manteiga, her version of a classic Genoise or butter sponge cake.

Her notes were spare and unclear, her technique unorthodox. I tested this recipe more times than I have any other; the results tasted great but had too dense a texture and dried out in the course of a day.

But here, with help from numerous sources, including Marion Cunningham's "Baking" and kikalicious.com, is the recipe that yielded a perfect result first time!

A true sponge cake contains no baking powder or fat but this richer, less airy version is well known in the Iberian Peninsula and in France. The texture is firm but light, and the flavor is all cake. It cuts clean, without crumbs, making it perfect for decorative uses. And it's known for its ability to soak up spirits, as with the butter cakes used in English trifle.

Some tips:

- As with all baking in Hawai'i, unless your kitchen is climate-controlled, work in the cool of the morning.

- Pão de Ló Manteiga can be baked in a conventional cake pan or baking dish, or, for in a rimmed baking sheet, which produces bar cookie-thin pieces. See note below on pans I used.

- Well-wrapped in plastic wrap, this cake can be refrigerated for a couple of days or frozen for up to a month. Defrost in refrigerator, then remove to room temperature. This cake should be used on the first day of baking or wrapped and chilled or frozen as soon as it's cool.

- Melt butter over very low heat; 3 on a scale of 10. Cool to lukewarm.

- Grandma used cornstarch to lighten the flour, mimicking cake flour, but this is not necessary.

- When adding the whites, fold, don't stir. Push the batter as far to one side of the bowl as possible, Scoop a ladle or two of whites into the empty space and lift batter to cover the whites, progressively incorporating them without cutting through or flattening the whites.

- This versatile cake, the base of many dessert creations, is often dressed in unconventional ways. In Portugal, it might be baked in a wide, flat dish or pan, brushed with Port or Madeira while still warm, served with sweet crushed fruit and a dusting of confectioners' sugar or dollop of whipped cream. Round cakes can be filled with jam or chopped fresh or softened dried fruit mixed with conventional frosting and topped with whipped cream. Or just fill and frost as you would any other cake.

1 stick (8 ounces) butter
8 eggs
Pinch of salt
1⅓ cups flour
2 teaspoons baking powder
1 cup plus 3 tablespoons
**   sugar**
Optional: 1 generous tea-
**   spoon vanilla or lemon**
**   extract**

Butter sponge cake, stacked with pureéd cherry pie filling.

Optional: Madeira, Port,
Sherry or other spirits for brushing while cake is warm

Preheat oven to 350°F. Prepare two 8-by-10-inch rimmed baking sheets or one large jelly roll pan* with grease and flour in the old-fashioned way or oil-and-flour baking spray (a product also known as "baking release").

Melt butter over low heat and set aside to cool; it will thicken to a creamy sludge.

(continued on the next page)

Separate eggs: whites in mixing bowl and yolks in small bowl. In a stand mixer or using a hand-held mixer, beat egg whites with salt to soft peaks. Set aside.

In a medium mixing bowl, whisk or sift together flour and baking powder. Set aside.

In a stand mixer or using a hand-held mixer, cream yolks, sugar and extract, if using, until lightened and thickened (it will be a lovely cream color, like vanilla frosting). Beating on low, slowly add cooled butter "sludge" to yolk-sugar mixture. Remove from stand or set aside mixture. Lighten the mixture with a third-cup or so of egg white, folding it in by hand (wooden spoon or rubber spatula).

Alternately fold in flour-baking powder mixture with egg whites, mixing in an up-and-over, up-and-under motion very gently. Do not stir in a circulation motion. Carefully pour into prepared pan(s), leveling the top with a rubber spatula.

Bake 25 minutes until golden and knife inserted into center emerges clean. Start checking at 20 minutes; the cake can quickly dry. Remove pan to heat-proof surface and allow to cool 5 minutes before turning cake out onto a rack. Cool completely.

At this point, the cake can be used in desired manner, wrapped well in plastic wrap and refrigerated or frozen up to 3 months. If frozen, defrost in refrigerator overnight and then at room temperature.

Makes 2 (8 × 10-inch) rectangles. Cut into squares, rounds, diamonds; fill and stack as desired.

Tip: I special-ordered small, rimmed baking pans (8 × 10-inch) for this job; some recipes specify 8 × 12-inch. You can use two 8 × 8-inch square cake pans or a shallow, disposable foil party tray. Shallow pans or rimmed baking sheets work best because the batter should be just a half-inch or so deep and won't bake properly in too deep a pan.

"If you don't like vinegar, you're not Portuguese."

—*Haroldine Nunes Garcia*

Temperos e Salsas
SEASONINGS, SAUCES AND BASE RECIPES

These are the building blocks of Portuguese cooking; without them, the cooking is plain, repetitive and ... well ... not really Portuguese. They infuse the dishes in this book with flavor and link them to Terra Velho, the "old country."

Molho de Piri Piri
PORTUGUESE CHILI PASTE

The chili sauce of Portugal is more evidence of the nation's maritime history. The name is Swahili for "pepper-pepper," the root of the term for African birds-eye chilies and the sauce made with them.

Due to my grandmother's delicate palate, we never made chili sauce. It was a revelation when I discovered in my 20s that Portuguese food could be spicy—in fact, should be spicy. Now I have a jar of Molho de Piri Piri in my refrigerator at all times.

Note that piri piri will eat through metal and infuse plastic; if you use a jar with a metal lid, place plastic wrap over the top before covering.

> **12 small, hot red Hawaiian chili peppers (ni'oi)**
> **2 teaspoons kosher salt**
> **1½ cups olive oil**
> **½ cup cider vinegar**

Pick off the green stems and puree the whole in a blender or food processor with a few drops olive oil. It is essential to puree or chop the chilies very finely; large bits catch unpleasantly in the throat. Some recipes call for garlic or lemon juice, as well—3 to 5 cloves of garlic, the juice of one or two lemons. In a sterile, airtight canning jar, combine the paste with additional olive oil, up to 1½ cups total (more olive oil, more sauce, slightly less heat). Cover and allow to season at room temperature for one week. Refrigerate thereafter; lasts forever.

Fiery piri piri chili sauce is generally served on the side, so diners can calibrate their own level of heat.

Tip: Wear kitchen gloves when working with chilies and never touch eyes, nose or other sensitive parts.

PORTUGUESE 5-SPICE

Everyone's heard of Chinese 5-Spice, but the Portuguese employ such a mixture, too. As Portuguese explorers ventured throughout Asia, there may have been some crossover that resulted in this warm and slightly sweet mixture.

How do they differ? Chinese: star anise, cloves, Szechuan pepper, cinnamon, fennel. Portuguese: Cinnamon, cloves, peppercorns, bay leaves, star anise.

Families would share the cost of ingredients and the work of gathering fresh bay, then roast the whole spices in the forno and divide the result. This recipe is for just such a large batch and requires a coffee grinder dedicated to spices or a large mortar and pestle or blender; the food processor isn't suitable. Shortcut versions follow.

1 bottle cinnamon sticks *
1 bottle whole cloves *
1 bottle whole black peppercorns *
Handful fresh bay leaves (sold at farmers markets)
Handful whole star anise

Preheat oven to 300°F. In a rimmed baking sheet, mix all ingredients and spread in a single layer. Toast until crisp and aromatic. Finely grind. Store in airtight containers (empty spice bottles work well).

*The bottles called for are the standard (not the large) size found in grocery stores, which, depending on the spice, range in weight from .5 ounces to 1.5 ounces.

Shortcut variation: Combine equal parts ground cinnamon, cloves, pepper and bay leaf; grind a whole star anise in a stone or marble mortar and pestle. (If you can't find ground bay leaf, use the mortar and pestle there, too.)

Quick soup or stew variation: Tie up in cheesecloth or a cloth tea bag 1 whole cinnamon stick, 2 cloves, 2 star anise, 1 or 2 bay leaves and 3 to 4 peppercorns and immerse in soup or stew while cooking.

Cebolada
ONION SAUCE

This sauce was a favorite in our household with fried liver. You don't see liver and onions on menus much anymore, but this sauce also works wonderfully with grilled or fried fish, chicken or pork.

- ¼ cup olive oil
- 6 medium yellow onions or sweet onions, very thinly sliced
- 5 cloves garlic, minced
- ¼ cup white wine vinegar
- ¼ cup water
- ¼ to ½ teaspoon salt
- ¼ cup fresh parsley, chopped

In a heavy-bottomed pot, such as a Dutch oven, heat oil over medium heat and sweat onions slowly, turning heat down if they show any sign of beginning to brown. They should be translucent and limp after half an hour. Add garlic and cook until golden but not browned. Stir in vinegar and water; add salt and taste. Finish with parsley.

Variation: Add a few drops Molho de Piri Piri (see page 36) to spice up the sauce.

Salsa Limão
LEMON SAUCE
Makes about 1 cup

This old-fashioned sauce uses egg yolks for thickening, a practice that has gone a bit out of favor but that deserves a revival. Try this with fried chicken or steamed vegetables.

4 egg yolks
2 tablespoons flat-leaf parsley, minced
Juice and zest of 1 large or 2 smaller lemons
½ cup water
1 tablespoon cornstarch
Salt to taste
Pinch of black or white pepper
Thinly sliced lemon, for garnish

In a bowl, whisk together yolks and parsley. Stir in juice and zest. In a small bowl or a measuring cup, using a mini-whisk or fork, whisk together water and cornstarch to make a slurry. Add slurry to lemon mixture and pour all into saucepan. Cook, stirring, over medium-low heat until glazed and thickened. Add salt and pepper; taste and correct seasonings. Serve warm or at room temperature.

Salsa Verde
PARSLEY SAUCE

This cold sauce is meant to be drizzled over anything from steamed potatoes to boiled octopus. The flavor is bright and piquant and can be spicy or not, as you wish.

2 cloves garlic, chopped
1 bunch flat-leaf parsley, minced
1 small hot red Hawaiian chili peppers (ni'oi), seeded and minced (optional)
¼ cup white vinegar
1 cup olive oil
¼ to ½ teaspoon EACH salt and pepper, or to taste

With a mortar and pestle or using a mini-processor or the back of a spoon, mash garlic, parsley and chili (if using) until fully incorporated into a paste. In a small bowl, combine garlic-parsley mixture with vinegar and olive oil and whisk. Season with salt and pepper; taste and correct seasoning. Store at room temperature and stir or shake before use.

Variation: Some versions of this sauce use a peeled, boiled, mashed salad potato as a base.

Vinha d'ahlos
PICKLING MARINADE

Years ago, I donated a five-course Portuguese dinner to a charity event. About the third course, I overheard one of the tipsy guests slur, "Are we going to have vinegar in every course?" The answer: If it's a Portuguese meal, yes, there'll be vinegar or sharp white wine in or on everything except dessert.

A favorite use for vinegar is vinha d'ahlos (veen-ya d'AH-lsh; for some reason islanders insist on veen-ya d'OY-lsh, which translates roughly as "pickled eyes.") It is used to pickle almost anything, from raw onions to tiny fried fish.

A Portuguese woman cooking vinha d'ahlos.

Recipes vary: Different measures of garlic or chilies, or different spices. Dry white wine for part of the vinegar or cider vinegar instead of white. Some people dilute the marinade with water to make it less puckery.

> 3 cups white vinegar
> 2 tablespoons Hawaiian or kosher salt
> 3 to 5 cloves garlic, mashed
> 4 to 6 small red Hawaiian chili peppers (ni'oi), finely chopped

Combine all ingredients in a non-reactive bowl (preferably glass or ceramic). Meats are marinated, covered, at room temperature overnight; fish needs just an hour or so in the mixture.

PICKLED ONIONS
Makes 2 to 3 quart jars

J ust as every Chinese home in my childhood had a gallon jar on the roof of the carport full of pickled lemon, every Portuguese household had an old quart jar or ceramic crock on the kitchen counter full of pickled onions. Grandpa would walk by, fish out a piece with his fingers (drove Grandma nuts!) and walk out to the garden, munching.

This recipe can also be used with carrots, cauliflower, pipinellas (chayote squash) and other vegetables, but in those cases, can the mixture in a 15-minute hot water bath for safety, or keep it refrigerated and use within a week or so.

2 to 3 sweet onions (such as Maui or Vidalia)
2 to 3 red bell peppers
3 to 6 small, red Hawaiian chili peppers (niʻoi)
1½ cups white vinegar
1½ cups water
1 tablespoon Hawaiian salt
2 teaspoons pickling spice

Cut onions into eighths and break the chunks apart. Quarter bell peppers, scrape out seeds and membranes and cut into thin strips. Wearing kitchen gloves, break off stems from chilies and lightly press to smash gently, retaining any seeds that escape. Layer onions, bell pepper strips and chili peppers in 2 to 3 sterilized glass jars, making sure each jar contains at least one chili.

In a nonreactive saucepan, combine vinegar, water, salt and pickling spice. Bring to a boil. Carefully pour hot liquid over onions and peppers in jars until liquid fills to within ½-inch of top. Cover the top with plastic wrap or decorative cellophane; cap the jars tightly and marinate at least 24 hours before serving. May be left at room temperature or refrigerated. Serve as pūpū with beer, as a complement to grilled fish and meats, or in sandwich fillings.

Aperitivos
e De Manha

FIRST COURSES AND
FIRST MEALS

I n Portuguese cities, meals almost always begin with nibbles. Wine bars and taverns may serve nothing but small
plates. In the country, nibbles are generally reserved for
special occasions, or are the province of men—who chomp
nuts and salted beans while they play cards, drink wine and
trade stories. (The women, one assumes, are in the kitchen,
eating leftovers and having an equally good time gossiping.)

BOM DIA

A word about the Portuguese breakfast: It is, unless you've got 10 hours of farm work to do, a continental breakfast: crusty rolls, coffee, a sliver of cheese or ham, jam, perhaps some fruit.

As in Spain, a favorite of city Portuguese is quince jam with white cheese. And like the Italians, they might spike their cafe with something strong, such as brandy. Or even have a glass of wine. (Not the practice, I hasten to add, in my family home.)

For working men of old Hawai'i, however, breakfast was something hot, often liquid, and easy to eat before they rushed out before the 5:30 a.m. whistle. Some reheated soup with old bread (old Portuguese white bread is hard enough to hurt someone if they hit you with it).

Grandpa loved sopas de cafe: hot coffee in an immense, bowl-like cup, about half of which was "canned cream" (evaporated milk), served with day-old bread or Saloon Pilot crackers broken into the coffee.

On special days, eggs were almost always scrambled with lots of parsley. There might be linguiça or ham, but rarely bacon. Grandpa liked sardines, quickly broiled or fried.

On blessed weekends there might be pão doce (sweetbread) with lots of butter (or in our thrifty house, margarine) and guava jelly.

Fried bread is also a favorite—slices fried until golden in a thin slick of melted bacon fat, other meat drippings, or in plain lard. Slip an egg on top and serve piping hot.

Portuguese raised chickens, gathered eggs daily and loved anything egg: omelets, scrambled eggs and especially egg custards and eggy cakes.

Ovos Batidos a Madeira
PORTUGUESE SCRAMBLED EGGS WITH ROASTED TOMATOES
Makes 4 to 6 servings

Roasting tomatoes draws out bright flavors; here, they pair with scrambled eggs."

1 basket cherry or grape tomatoes
½ bell pepper (green, red or yellow), seeded, trimmed and chopped into tiny squares
1 teaspoon sugar
1 teaspoon salt
2 tablespoons olive oil
7 eggs
¼ cup milk or half-and-half (non-fat okay) or cream
¼ teaspoon pepper
Olive oil spray
1 teaspoon salt
Hot buttered toast or fried bread

Preheat oven to 450°F. Line a rimmed baking sheet with nonstick aluminum foil. Cut cherry or grape tomatoes in half and place each, cut-side-up, on half the baking sheet. Scatter bell pepper on the other half. The goal is to expose the surface of every piece to the heat. In a small bowl or measuring cup, mix together sugar and salt and sprinkle lightly over vegetables, covering evenly. Drizzle olive oil slowly over vegetables. Roast until tomatoes are shriveled, bell pepper is soft and both are lightly browned around the edges.

In a bowl, whisk together eggs, milk (or half-and-half or cream), salt and pepper. Spray a large saute pan with olive oil spray and heat over medium heat. Pour in eggs, reduce heat to medium and cook eggs 1 to 2 minutes; add tomatoes and bell pepper and scramble lightly just until eggs are softly set. Serve over hot buttered toast or fried bread.

Bolinhos De Atom e Broa
CORNBREAD-TUNA CAKES
Makes 4 servings

1 loaf broa (yeasted cornbread; see Breads chapter, page 166) or other savory (not sweet) cornbread, crumbled to make 2 cups
¼ cup cilantro (Chinese parsley), minced
¼ cup flat-leaf parsley, minced
3 large eggs, lightly beaten
3 (5-ounce each) cans tuna, drained
3 tablespoons mayonnaise
1 teaspoon garlic powder
2 tablespoons EACH butter and olive oil
Condiments: Ketchup, chutney, piri piri (page 36), aioli (garlic mayonnaise)

In a bowl, combine crumbled cornbread, cilantro, flat-leaf parsley, eggs, tuna, mayonnaise and garlic powder. Shape into patties. (If not frying right away, cover and refrigerate.) In a large saute pan over medium-high heat, heat together butter and olive oil. Fry tuna-cornbread patties until golden on one side; turn and finish other side.

BACALHAO • SALT COD: CURRENCY AND CONSOLATION

acalhao (bah-kahl-YOW), salt cod, has a storied history among the peoples of the Atlantic and the southern Mediterranean. In the 1400s, salt cod came to be valued as the perfect ship's store: high in protein, light in weight, space-saving, long-lasting, resistant to spoilage or infestation.

Thus, cod became a form of maritime currency, and one leg of several phenomenally profitable trading routes. Cod is a broad term covering the 60 species of the long, narrow, full-bodied, finned fish called *gadidae*. Cod are prolific, can grow to immense size (in excess of 200 pounds) and are lean, white-fleshed and flaky.

Cod were waiting when the first long-distance fishing ships piloted by peoples we lump together as Vikings reached the North Atlantic in the 1200s. It is likely that the first Europeans who set foot on American soil originally set out on a search for cod.

The cod fishing industry grew as industrialization brought a need for portable foods, especially for selling in cities. In 1497, a Venetian, Giovanni Cabato, on a voyage of discovery under letters patent from Henry VII of England, "discovered" the Grand Banks. There, he found fish so plentiful it was said that you could scoop them up in buckets. This abundance continued for hundreds of years. "He is a very bad fisherman who cannot kill in one day 200 to 300 cod," wrote John Smith in 1616.

Boats setting out with the combined goal of hauling in fish and discovering new land would sail from Portugal and England to Newfoundland and Iceland, where they'd catch fish literally until their vessels almost foundered. These would be cleaned, butterflied, salted and stacked in neat bundles belowdecks from floor to ceiling. After a few days the ships would find a rocky shore and spread the fish to dry before packing them with more salt in empty barrels or boxes. This was bacalhao, so heavily salted most of us would find it unpalatable today even after rinsing and boiling, and so hard you could use it as a weapon. The word is said to mean "weapon," specifically, a whip with which to lash slaves.

The cod could be sold in Europe, or to other vessels. The American colonies paid some taxes in cod. Ships in need purchased cod from other ships at sea with gold.

Our great-grandparents paid pennies for entire sides of hard-salted cod, hung from hooks above the counters of fish shops. You really could hurt someone with one, if you'd a mind to; they were hard and wide as lacrosse sticks.

We ate them in tomato-based oniony thick stews, liberally drenched in a vinegar, garlic and flat-leaf parsley marinade and quick-fried, laced into creamy sauces. Feed one of these dishes to an elder Portuguese. Bet you a box of cod their response is: Consolo! (koon-SOH-lo; comforting, soul-satisfying.)

Bolinhos De Bacalhao
SALT COD CROQUETTES
Makes 4 to 6 pūpū-size servings

In Portugal, you're served these crunchy outside/creamy inside croquettes everywhere. Our family, like many in Hawai'i, made them for holidays. I like them as flat cakes in a sandwich with aioli (garlic mayonnaise).

> 2½ cups dry bread cubes OR stiff, plain mashed potatoes
>   (no butter or cream)
> 12 ounces salt cod*
> 3 eggs
> 1 small onion, minced or grated
> 4 tablespoons flat-leaf parsley, chopped
> 2 tablespoons cilantro (or more), chopped
> Paprika and pepper to taste
> Olive oil
> Optional garnishes: Olives, pickled onions, piri piri, aioli

If you're using bread chunks, place in a bowl and drizzle ¼ cup olive oil over the bread and mash the bread well. In a large bowl, beat eggs and add salt cod, dry bread or mashed potatoes, onion, parsley, cilantro and a pinch of paprika and a few sprinkles of pepper. Toss to combine. The mixture should be rather stiff, neither dry nor too liquid. If it's too loose, add more bread or mashed potatoes. With two spoons, form small discs, spheres or football shapes; set aside on a sheet of waxed paper or a flat plate or rimmed baking sheet lined with parchment paper. If you're not planning to serve the bolinhos immediately, refrigerate them, loosely covered with plastic wrap.

Place a thin slick of olive oil or vegetable oil in a large saute pan, heat over medium high. Brown cakes, not crowding them, 3 to 4 minutes per side. Serve at once.

*Prepared according to Salt Cod Technique, page 114

PORTUGUESE CHICKEN "POKE"

Makes 8 to 10 pūpū servings or 4 to 6 mini-meals with rice

I made this dish up—a cooked poke featuring Portuguese ingredients, most of them lightly cooked. Using skin-on, bone-in chicken thighs assures a moist result. Roasting it with fresh rosemary infuses the meat with taste without overwhelming its flavor; if you use dried rosemary, do so sparingly. And if you're really rushed, use store-bought grilled or poached chicken—marinate it, pat it dry, cut it into chunks and use as directed.

5 to 6 bone-in, skin-on chicken thighs
½ cup cider vinegar
1 tablespoon brown sugar
1 small, hot red chili pepper, finely minced (do not seed)
4 tablespoons olive oil, divided use
1 large red onion, coarsely chopped
3 cloves garlic, chopped
Salt and pepper
4 to 5 long sprigs fresh rosemary (or ground, dried rosemary to taste)
1 basket cherry tomatoes, halved
½ cup green onion (green and white parts), thinly sliced

Pierce chicken thighs with a knife in several places. In a bowl, marinate chicken in cider vinegar with brown sugar and chili pepper for 30 minutes. Meanwhile, in a large saute pan, heat 2 tablespoons olive oil and caramelize onion and garlic over medium-low heat just until partially cooked, 3 to 4 minutes; onion should still be a little crunchy. Drain on paper towels and reserve.

Preheat oven to 350°F. Place 2 tablespoons olive oil in a shallow baking dish; drain chicken thighs well and pat dry. Rub chicken generously with salt and pepper. Place rosemary sprigs on the bottom of the baking dish and arrange the chicken on top. Roast 30 to 40 minutes, until chicken is cooked through (145°F on an instant-read thermometer). Remove chicken and cool until you can handle it; remove skin, bone thighs and cut chicken meat into poke-size chunks.

(continued on the next page)

In a serving bowl, lightly toss together all ingredients. Serve as you would fish poke or over hot rice as a mini-meal.

Variations: Use raw onion and garlic and reduce olive oil to 2 tablespoons for roasting chicken. Use chopped Portuguese pickled onions (see page 42).

SARDINE EGG SPREAD
Makes 6 to 10 pūpū servings

Grandpa's favorite thing was sardines: grilled, mashed with tuna salad or, occasionally, in a tomatoey egg salad like this one. I never got the recipe from Grandma, but this one, with the addition of tomatoes (an idea I borrowed from Italy), fits my taste memory.

> 1 dozen hard-boiled eggs, peeled and sliced in half
> 2 tablespoons sweet onion, minced very fine (or grated)
> 2 tablespoons flat-leaf parsley, minced (plus more for garnish)
> 1 (14.5-ounce) can chopped tomatoes, drained, chopped
>   more finely
> 1 clove garlic, minced
> 1 teaspoon coarse Dijon mustard
> ½ teaspoon black pepper
> ½ cup mayonnaise
> 1 (4.5-ounce) can sardines, drained and finely chopped

Remove the egg yolks from the whites. Arrange the whites on a serving plate. In a bowl, combine onion, parsley, tomatoes, garlic, mustard, pepper, mayonnaise and sardines. Mix well and fill egg white halves. Garnish with minced parsley.

Variation: Instead of stuffing egg whites, chop them and add to mixture and serve atop toast rounds or crackers. Omit sardines; substitute 2 tablespoons anchovy paste. Or use 2 (5-ounce) cans well-drained tuna and anchovy paste.

STUFFED FIGS

Makes 6 pūpū servings

Portuguese make many cheeses, none of which are available here. Among substitutes for their soft, white queijos frescos or requeijao (fresh sheep or goat cheese or farmer's cheese) is French-style chevre. Or, if you're able to get it where you live, use Oʻahu-made Naked Cow Dairy farm cheese.

12 dried figs
½ cup soft chevre-style goat
cheese or chunks of
farm cheese
2 teaspoons Madeira
wine, sherry or port
Pinch of black pepper
12 salty fried almonds (see note)

Cut a slit in each fig lengthwise from bottom to just short of stem, leaving top attached so the fig opens up in a "V" shape. In a small bowl, if using a soft cheese, combine cheese, wine black pepper. Using a pastry bag or a funnel of parchment paper, fill each fig with cheese mixture and press a salty fried almond into each. If using a slightly harder cheese, cut it into chunks, crumble, lightly pepper the cheese and place inside the figs; top with nut.

To make toasted almonds: Simmer 12 whole almonds in water 10 minutes. Drain and rub almonds in a towel to remove skins. Spread out to dry on a paper towel. In a saute pan, heat a thin slick of olive oil, fry almonds over medium heat, stirring or flipping until golden. Remove to a plate and season lightly with sea salt. Can be served as is or add a light sprinkle of Portuguese 5-Spice (page 37) OR a grind or two of ground black pepper and 1 teaspoon Molho de Piri Piri (page 36) and toss well.

Camãrao Pica
SPICY SHRIMP
Makes 4 to 6 pūpū or first-course servings

S hrimps swimming in olive oil, flecked with garlic and lemon, this is my favorite shellfish recipe and the Portuguese-style appetizer I turn to most often. You need peeled but tail-on shrimp; frozen is OK. Be sure to choose the best quality artisanal bread. This goes together very fast, so don't start it until all the guests have arrived.

    1 cup extra virgin olive oil
    3 cloves garlic, minced
    Juice and zest of 1 lemon
    1 teaspoon flaked sea salt
    $1/2$ teaspoon coarse-ground black pepper
    1 to 2 pounds peeled, tail-on raw shrimp (18-20 count or
      larger)
    Warm crusty country-style bread
    Molho de Piri Piri (Portuguese Chili Paste, page 36)

Place olive oil in a heavy-bottomed deep frying pan or Dutch oven; heat over medium-high heat until very hot but not smoking. Meanwhile, combine garlic, lemon juice and zest, salt and pepper and rub shrimp with this mixture. Place seasoned shrimp in oil and cook, spooning hot oil over as needed, just until pink—no longer! Serve immediately in warmed shallow bowls, 3 to 5 shrimp per bowl, each swimming in a pool of oil. Serve immediately with piri piri for drizzling over and bread for dipping.

Torresmos
FRIED PORK BITES
Makes 10 to 12 breakfast or pūpū servings

The key here is to dry the pork thoroughly and fry it (not boil it in its juices). Stovetop frying often dried out the meat; this oven method leaves the pork moist.

Torresmos can be made from leftover roast vinha d'ahlos pork, cut into chunks. Don't cut the chunks too small; they should be at least 1¼ inches on a side because they shrink.

1 (4-pound) boneless pork butt

For the marinade:
8 to 10 small, hot, red Hawaiian chili peppers (niʻoi), stemmed
1 tablespoon salt
4 tablespoons paprika, sweet or hot, but not smoked
10 cloves garlic, chopped
½ cup white wine or sherry
¼ cup red wine
1 cup white or cider vinegar

For frying:
Vegetable oil or lard for oven-frying
½ teaspoon salt
¼ teaspoon pepper
Sprinkle of paprika

Cut pork butt into chunks, trimming excess fat and any gristle. Place in a large, non-reactive bowl or container with cover.

Mince chili peppers and place in a medium bowl with remaining marinade ingredients; still well and pour over pork. Cover and marinate 24 hours.

Remove the pork from the marinade, discarding marinade. Drain the pork and press between paper towels. Better yet, air-dry pork on paper towels in refrigerator until close to serving time.

Pour ½-inch oil in a large roasting pan; place in 375°F oven. Meanwhile, season pork well with salt, pepper and a sprinkle of paprika. When the oil is hot, add pork and roast, turning to brown all sides (do not poke or prod or turn more than once per side); after 30 minutes, check pork temperature (145°F on an instant-read thermometer). Pork should be slightly crispy and browned on all sides. Serve hot on a bed of greens with toothpicks or with scrambled eggs and good bread for breakfast.

Although presented here as an appetizer, this is the dish most Portuguese remember as Christmas-morning breakfast (a meal that often came at 2 AM, after midnight Mass) or day-after-Christmas breakfast, when leftover vinha d'ahlos pork roast would be fried to serve with eggs, bread and olives.

GREEN PAPAYA PICKLE
Makes 4 to 6 pūpū servings

Portuguese often used green papaya as a vegetable, as a tenderizer for meats, or in pickles. Use the green papaya sold in Filipino, Vietnamese or Thai outlets, not an unripe table papaya. This particularly complements grilled fish or fried Portuguese sausage.

1 green ("cooking") papaya
Water
1 small sweet onion, sliced fine
1 teaspoon salt
2 teaspoons sugar
¼ cup white vinegar (or use cider or Filipino-style palm
   vinegar)

Peel papaya, halve and remove seeds and strings. Cut into small chunks (¼-inch dice). Place papaya in saucepan with water to cover and bring to a boil; boil 2 minutes. Drain well and pat dry with paper towels. Toss with onion, salt, sugar and vinegar and serve as a pupu or atop grilled fish.

GRILLED ABALONE PORTUGUEZA
Makes 4 servings

Portuguese love mollusks, snails and other shelled sea creatures. Many can remember when abalone were cheap (well, free, really because most people dove for their own). Do not substitute canned "Top Shell" for abalone in this recipe.

Farm-raised abalone from Big Island Abalone has become available at farmers markets and online (www.bigislandabalone.com). They ain't cheap. If you decide to dig deep and use abalone, plan on it as a tiny, select first course of two per person.

2 tablespoons sweet onion, finely minced
2 tablespoons flat-leaf parsley, finely minced
1 tablespoon cilantro stems, finely minced
1 tablespoon cilantro leaves, finely minced
2 ripe beefsteak tomatoes, finely chopped
Juice and zest of 1 lemon
Juice and zest of 1 orange
1 tablespoon minced macadamia nuts or chopped pine nuts
Drizzle of fruity olive oil
Sea salt and freshly ground pepper to taste
8 cleaned Big Island abalone in bottom shell

Combine sauce ingredients (everything but abalone) to make a salsa. Preheat grill to white ash stage, or 450°F on gas grill. In a large bowl under cold running water, rinse abalone, drain on paper towels. Place shell-side-down on grill (you'll eat them from the shell). Spoon a little salsa over each abalone. When abalone begins to bubble in shell, remove and arrange 2 per plate and drizzle artfully with remaining salsa. Serve immediately as an appetizer.

Sopas
SOUPS

THE PORTUGUESE WAY WITH SOUPS

hen the famed cooking tome "Larousse Gastronomique" identified the attributes that characterize Portuguese cuisine, No. 2 of five points was "a marked taste for soups." The 1958 publication, "Racial Foods in Hawai'i" from the Hawai'i Bureau of Nutrition said, "The thick Portuguese soup is a one-dish meal with dried beans as a base, salt pork or pig's tail as seasoning and all available vegetables added. Watercress or kale are often added just before serving. A huge cauldron of soup is prepared and eaten at any or all meals until finished."

There are obvious reasons for this "marked taste": large families, little money and mothers with much to do, including, in some cases, working a plantation shift. Soup could be heated and reheated and needed little tending. It could be cooked in the residual heat of the forno (the beehive-shaped masonry oven in which bread was baked), saving fuel. It used up leftovers, from stale bread to aging vegetables. And, as Grandma always said, if somebody drops by, "just add more water."

It was actually rather difficult to tease out recipes for this chapter, because who used recipes to make soup? You made broth with whatever meat on the bone you had, or with tomatoes, onions or potatoes when there was no meat. You looked in the garden, you looked in the pantry, you took whatever your neighbor had brought over or you'd bartered for that day and you made soup. A careful housewife always had some means of making soup.

MAKING SOUP WITH GRANDMA

It is April 1985, and I have begun to test recipes for the Portuguese-Hawai'i book I have always wanted to write. We are on vacation at a home in the country, a rundown, wood-floored, many-windowed structure with glass-fronted kitchen cabinets that remind me of Grandma's Main Street Wailuku home.

I began as our grandmothers would have: I soak two pounds of dried red beans in a pot of water just before bed. The next morning, I pulled out half a cut onion, an aging carrot, some just-over-the-hill parsley, the dried-up hulk of half a kabocha pumpkin and two ham hocks and threw them in a pot. Brought the pot to a boil, skimmed, lowered the heat to simmer. The beans, drained, went into another pot of water to simmer until tender. Sat down to write.

I smiled to myself, metaphorically feeling Grandma's worn house slippers on my feet. I was actually wearing one of her old aprons. She would have scolded me for all the times I have let ingredients die in the back recesses of the refrigerator. As with any homemaker of her time, she kept a running inventory in her head of the contents of her refrigerator, and could review it with the speed and accuracy of a computer, planning menus to make use of these otherwise doomed ingredients.

How pleasurable to have this kind of competence and control over a task. It is a thing I long for and the reason I love cooking so much. There is nothing in my complex, over-busy, electronics-driven professional life of which I am so sure.

Not that I don't make mistakes. But they are private and usually fixable. And so many people today are awed by anyone who knows how to do more than cruise the frozen hors d'oeuvre aisle at Costco that I get away with my flubs.

I lack two key features possessed by all great cooks: Patience and what Grandma might have called "The Sight." I cannot keep myself from poking or turning a piece of frying fish or meat. I open the oven on cakes too soon. I cannot accurately envision a dish in advance, I have to fumble around with actual ingredients, test them out, learn by doing.

In any case, on this day, I wasn't making soup; I was making a stock. Stock is the heart of any good soup and if it's weak, salty, bitter or otherwise flawed, the soup won't work.

People often say, "Oh, you just throw everything in and walk away." Not so. Even if it's how they said they did, our grandmothers instinctively did things you don't find written in their recipe books. They may have used somewhat tired vegetables or herbs, but they used the meatiest soup bones they could find; they used ham hocks, slicing from the fatty cured skin through to the meaty bone to release the goodness inside. They dug into bones for marrow. They boiled once, skimmed, turned the heat down and simmered gently.

Adelaide "Ida" H. Sylva
Waiheʻe, Maui ca. 1915 (about age 20)

They added like-textured ingredients in layers, hard vegetables first. They prepared little bundles or bags of aromatics. They let the stock cool and skimmed the fat. They strained it through layers of cheesecloth. They never covered simmering stock, though they would loosely cover soup. They'd mash some beans to thicken the soup.

They had this knowledge in their hands, not their heads. And they assumed everyone with any sense would employ the same instinctual understanding.

It's fashionable these days to say that much of the hunger for old recipes is just nostalgia; a craving for the people and feelings that surrounded the dishes we ate, not the dishes themselves. I agree. But I think the food was pretty darned good, too; I don't think our memories lie. We're just not willing, or don't have the time, to take the steps that our grandparents did to recreate those flavors. When you do so—it's uncanny—the memories and the people come back, too. If only for a few moments at table.

SOUP STOCK
Makes 6 to 8 cups

My grandmother and mother would both be millionaires if only they had a nickel for every time they said, "We come from strong stock!"

Well, so does good soup. Here's a recipe for all-purpose stock. Gone are the days when you could get the butcher to throw in bones for free, so buy bone-in meat parts in bulk when they are on rock-bottom sale. Then, on a weekend, make stock and freeze it. Freeze some in ice cube trays, then seal in plastic bags for when you need just a little. And, I blush to say this, but the boxed, shelf-stable organic beef and chicken broth available today ain't bad. And neither are the new concentrated stocks that come in tiny tubs or packets.

> **2 to 3 pounds chicken parts OR meaty pork bones with a knob of salt pork or a ham hock OR 2 to 3 pounds meaty beef soup bones***
> **1 bay leaf (more if they're dried, not fresh; find fresh in farmers markets)**
> **Handful of parsley stems OR bouquet garni of parsley, thyme and bay leaf**
> **1 cup onions, coarsely chopped**
> **½ cup carrot, peeled and chopped**
> **½ cup celery, chopped**
> **1 stalk leek, well washed, cut into 2-inch lengths**

Cover meats with cold water and bring to a boil; skim and reduce heat to simmer for 20 minutes. Add vegetables and herbs and simmer 1 to 2 hours, skimming as required. Strain and discard solids, pressing to release all liquid (though the ham hock, if used, can be frozen and used again). If there's time, refrigerate and skim off fat.

* If using chicken, first cut the chicken into joints, then use the back of a heavy cleaver to break the thick thigh bones.
** For darker stock, rub bones with olive oil, place on foil-lined baking sheet and roast at 450°F until dark. Then make stock.

PORTUGUESE BEAN SOUP

The national soup of Portugal is Caldo Verde ("Green Soup"). So how did bean soup become the only Portuguese soup that most people in Hawaiʻi know? I wish I knew. I wish somebody knew. I've been researching this for years, to find Portuguese bean soup in island cookbooks almost as far back as they go. I've asked every elder Portuguese I've ever met and all say their mothers or grandmothers made many soups—pearl barley, pumpkin, fish, soup with every protein and vegetable that came their way.

The late Mary Sylva of Maui suggested that bean soup might have gained popularity via the many Holy Ghost festivals held at Catholic churches. "When I was young, the only thing I knew about Japanese food was mochi because they had that at bon dance. And hekka, they taught it with the home economics ladies," she told me years ago. She thought fundraising sales were why people in Hawaiʻi think pão doce (sweetbread) is the only Portuguese bread and she applied the idea to bean soup.

It's a theory. And I've got no better explanation.

Important: Once greens are added to soup, they begin to gray and lose their crunch. Members of the *Brassicae* (cabbage) family can develop an off flavor and nasty smell. I suggest portioning out the soup to serve at a sitting, pouring off and refrigerating or freezing what you won't use that day, then re-heating to a gentle boil and adding the greens at the last minute. Portuguese cabbage (couves) or spinach take just minutes. Collard, head cabbage and kale need the most cooking.

Tip: To chop canned tomatoes, pour into a bowl and draw two sharp knives through them, working from center to outside.

PORTUGUESE SOUP THREE WAYS

My grandmother's bean soup was the scratchiest of the scratch: dried, not canned, kidney beans; stock made from soup bones and ham hocks; tomatoes and Portuguese cabbage from her own garden, frozen in "solid-pack." She also picked watercress she culti-vated in a nearby hanawai ditch. She was a bit of a purist: No macaroni. And never Portuguese sausage: too expensive!

PORTUGUESE SOUP: THE REAL THING

Makes 8 to 10 servings

2¼ cups dried red beans
1 to 2 pounds meaty soup bones
1 to 2 teaspoons olive oil
1 smoked ham hock
1 (28-ounce) can crushed tomatoes
½ bunch flat leaf parsley leaves, minced
2 to 3 cloves garlic, peeled and smashed
2 teaspoons Portuguese 5-Spice (see Temperos e Salsas, page 37)
2 pipinella (chayote) squash, cut into chunks
1 teaspoon salt
¼ teaspoon pepper
Dash or two of liquid hot pepper seasoning or chili pepper water, if desired
1 bunch Portugese cabbage, collard greens or kale, washed and chiffonade
Handful watercress leaves and tender stems

In a large bowl, cover dried beans with cold water and soak overnight. Or place in a pot, cover with water, bring to a boil and allow to soak overnight. The next day, drain and reserve beans. Preheat oven to 500°F. Rub soup bones with olive oil and roast in oven until dark brown. While bones are roasting, place ham hock in large, heavy-bottomed soup kettle with 6 cups cold water. Add roasted bones, bring to a boil over medium-high heat, then reduce heat to medium and simmer one hour. Remove soup bones, trim off any meat; return meat to soup and discard bones. Remove ham hock and discard (or freeze for one more use).

Add drained beans with 2 cups water; return to boil; skim foam and reduce heat to medium and simmer one hour. Add tomatoes, parsley, garlic, Portuguese spice and simmer 20 minutes; add pipinellas and simmer an additional 10 minutes. Taste and season with salt, pepper, hot sauce, if desired. Shortly before serving, bring soup to a gentle boil; add greens and watercress leaves and simmer just until they are bright green.

FROM-THE-PANTRY PORTUGUESE SOUP

Makes 8 bowls; 10 to 12 cups

This one-hour Portuguese soup is centered on ingredients that are always in my pantry, freezer, refrigerator and garden. Essentials include chopped cured meat (bacon or ham—or, if you must, Portuguese sausage), canned beans and tomatoes, flat-leaf parsley and, if at all possible, greens. Portuguese cabbage is traditional; collards or baby kale are a good substitute; watercress leaves, head cabbage or even spinach are fine. The combination of bacon and homemade Portuguese spice lends smokiness and a kind of exotic spiciness.

> 3 slices bacon, chopped
> ½ onion, sliced and broken into crescents
> Stems from 1 bunch flat-leaf parsley, tied with cotton string
> 1 (32-ounce) box beef broth
> 1 (28-ounce) can whole plum tomatoes, chopped, with juice
> 2 bay leaves (preferably fresh)
> 1 teaspoon Portuguese 5-Spice (see page 37)
> 3 cloves garlic, peeled and roughly chopped
> 2 (15.25-ounce) cans kidney beans, drained*
> 1 (6-ounce) can tomato paste
> Greens, about 2 cups julienned
> Leaves of ½ bunch flat-leaf parsley, chopped

In a heavy-bottomed soup kettle, fry bacon over medium-high heat until caramelized but not crisp. Add onion and parsley, fry until onion is translucent and limp. Add broth, plum tomatoes, bay leaves, Portuguese spice and garlic; bring to a boil. Reduce heat to medium and simmer 15 minutes. Measure ½ cup kidney beans and whirl in food processor or mini-processor or mash with fork (lumpy is OK); mash with tomato paste and add to soup along with remaining beans. Cook 15 minutes. (At this point, you can stop the cooking, refrigerate and continue later, if desired. Reheat over medium heat and begin.) Taste the soup. Shortly before serving, add greens and parsley leaves.

*For something different, use 1 can kidney beans and 1 can drained corn.

WIKIWIKI PORTUGUESE SOUP
Makes 6 to 8 servings

Don't have an hour? Don't make Portuguese soup. Oh, all right, here's a speed soup. And I'll even let you use macaroni in this one, if you want to.

Drizzle of olive oil
10 to 12 ounces Portuguese sausage, sliced
½ bunch flat-leaf watercress, minced
2 teaspoons bottled or fresh minced garlic
1 (28-ounce) crushed tomatoes
1 (32-ounce) box beef broth
2 (14.25-ounce) cans kidney beans, drained
1 to 2 cups cooked elbow macaroni (optional)
1 to 2 cups chopped greens (optional)
½ teaspoon salt
¼ teaspoon pepper
Dash or two of liquid hot pepper seasoning or chili pepper
   water, if desired

In a heavy-bottomed soup kettle, heat olive oil and fry Portugese sausage slices over medium-high heat just to brown the edges slightly. Add watercress and garlic and allow to wilt, stirring. Add tomatoes, beef broth and kidney beans. Bring to a boil. Reduce heat to medium, simmer 10 to 15 minutes. If the soup is too concentrated, thin with more broth or water. Add macaroni and greens, if using. Simmer 10 to 15 minutes more. Taste and season.

Tip: Buy large packages of bacon ends and repackage them into sandwich-size bags to store in the freezer when you need just a touch of pork flavor.

Açorda
BREAD SOUP
Makes 4 servings

Portuguese love bread and they're too thrifty to see it go to waste even after it's begun to get a bit tough on the teeth. So they make açordas (Ah-SOR-dahs) and migas (MEE-gahs), soups that can range from fine-textured to thick and stuffing-like. Grandma made this tomato-based bread-and-egg soup to use up stale bread. When I make it, I flavor the soup with bacon and coriander. (For Grandma's migas-style stuffing, see page 141).

¼ **cup bacon, chopped**
¼ **cup ham, chopped**
2 or 3 onions, chopped
4 cups beef broth
1 (15-ounce) can chopped tomatoes
Salt and pepper
8 cups dry, stale or toasted country-style bread, torn or
    cubed
4 eggs, lightly poached
Coriander powder

In the bottom of a soup pot, "melt" bacon and ham and saute onions over medium-low heat until limp and translucent. Add beef broth and tomatoes and simmer over medium heat until heated through; taste and add salt and pepper as needed. In four shallow open bowls, arrange bread chunks and divide half the broth evenly among the bowls, soaking the bread. Place a poached egg over bread in each bowl. Gently pour the remaining broth around the egg and over the bread. Sprinkle coriander over each bowl of soup. Serve hot.

Tip: To easily poach eggs, place in an oil-sprayed muffin tin. Place tin in a large saucepan or wok with water that comes about half-way up the sides of the muffin pan. Cover and simmer over medium heat until eggs are done to your liking.

REFOGADO: HEART OF THE STEW

I n Portuguese households, we gently heat the olive oil, throw in the onions and garlic, and then decide what we're going to cook: Because everything but dessert or bread starts with olive oil, onions and garlic! One thing we make frequently is refogado (ray-foh-ZHA-doo), a tomato base.

Many, many Portuguese dishes are built on tomatoes and many of these begin with a refogado. This quick, fresh tomato sauce is akin to the pomodoro of Italy, though more garlicky, lumpy with onions, tart-sweet with fresh tomatoes, much-used in both mainland Portugal and the Atlantic Islands.

Unfortunately, ripe, flavorful, beefsteak-type tomatoes are hard to come by in Hawai'i; tomatoes here are prey to many pests. Try farmers markets (stock up on the over-the-hill heirlooms when they're cheap, then peel, seed and freeze them). Or use canned.

Refogado freezes beautifully. Combine it with broth to make soup. Or add seafood—whole shrimp, squares of fish fillet, lump crab meat, mussels or scallops—to make a quick cioppino-type stew. Or stir in chunks of dredged and browned beef, carrots, potatoes or other root vegetables and/or steamed pumpkin, and beef stock to make a stew. Make a sauce for milho (cornmeal porridge) or pasta by adding herbs or Portuguese 5-Spice. Use it as is on grilled meats or fish. Or add a dab to other sauces, such as a bechamel (white sauce) or veloute (white sauce made with stock).

I call this formula Base Three.

BASE THREE

*I*t's important to use the best-tasting tomatoes you can get. If the only beefsteaks you can find are flavorless and have the texture of cardboard, use good-quality canned tomatoes. Local heirloom tomatoes are expensive but worth it, tomatoes sold on the vine will usually do.

12 large, ripe beefsteak toma-
    toes, stems trimmed out,
    left whole*
⅓ cup olive oil
2 large onions, peeled, thinly
    sliced, cut crosswise or
    roughly chopped
6 cloves garlic, minced

Bring a soup pot of water to a rolling boil and immerse tomatoes about 1 minute, until skins split. With a slotted spoon or wire ladle, life out tomatoes and place in colander to drain. When tomatoes are cool enough to touch, pull off skin, cut in half and squeeze to expel seeds. (You needn't capture every last seed, just the bulk of them.)

In a deep, heavy-bottomed pot, such as a Dutch oven, over medium heat, warm olive oil. Add prepared onions and garlic; stir and "sweat" 15-20 minutes to reduce and become golden, translucent and limp, stirring often and reducing heat at any sign of browning.

Add tomatoes and cook slowly, uncovered, over medium or medium-low heat until refogado is jammy and thickened, about 30 minutes. If the mixture is too thick or dominated by onions, add canned tomatoes as desired. If you prefer a less oniony, more tomatoey sauce, use 2 onions, add a cup or so of canned, puréed tomatoes.

Note: If you wish, place a bowl under the colander when you drain the tomatoes and capture the tomato water for other uses, such as salad dressing or chili peppah wattah.

*Have some canned tomato paste or puréed tomatoes on hand in case the sauce is too thin or weakly flavored.

BEEF-PUMPKIN-PIPINELLAS SOUP

This soup makes use of a vegetable we called pipinellas—better known as chayote squash and found in Southeast Asian and Mexican cooking, too. The potato-sized, pear-shaped, grooved white squash used to frustrate me as a child: I'd think I had found a potato in my soup or stew, but it would turn out to be a chunk of squash, which at the time I didn't like. Now, I like it.

- 2 pounds stew meat
- ⅔ cup flour well-seasoned with ½ teaspoon salt and ¼ teaspoon pepper, or to taste
- Olive or vegetable oil or rendered bacon fat—about 2 tablespoons, as needed to keep meat from sticking as it's browned
- 2 kabocha pumpkins (medium, about 1 to 1½ pounds each)
- 6 pipinellas (chayote squash)
- 1 small, hot, red chili pepper, stemmed and minced
- 2 teaspoons allspice
- 1 (28-ounce) can crushed tomatoes
- Water or beef stock (preferably homemade)
- 1 bunch kale, Portuguese cabbage or collard greens, julienned
- 2 (10-ounce) packages frozen lima beans

Dredge the stew meat in the seasoned flour. In the bottom of a heavy soup pot, heat oil or bacon fat and brown dredged stew meat; work in batches, if necessary; do not crowd the meat. As the meat browns, pierce the kabocha pumpkins in several places; microwave on high 7 to 10 minutes. Halve the pumpkin, scrape out seeds and strings; carve pumpkin from skin and cut into large chunks. Wash pipinellas well; pare away any stems or blemishes and cut into chunks (no need to skin but if you must, use a vegetable peeler and work around the rather challenging geography). Add to the meat and stir. Stir in chili and allspice along with tomatoes. Add broth or water to cover by at least a couple of inches. Bring to a boil; turn down heat and simmer until pumpkin and pipinellas are fork-tender and meat is cooked through. Add greens and lima beans. Simmer until all ingredients are cooked through and tender. Add salt to taste.

Tip: "Dredging" is a technique in which an ingredient, usually meat, is coated with seasoned flour before it is browned or braised. The flour mixture adds flavor, gives the meat a nice crust and thickens the soup.

Sopas Galinha a la Portugueza
PORTUGUESE-STYLE CHICKEN SOUP
Makes 6 to 8 servings

Grandma was never much for putting pasta in soup, but most Portuguese did so. Here, broken vermicelli combines with conventional chicken soup ingredients for a bowl of comfort. It resembles Midnight Soup, eaten after Midnight Mass on Christmas Day.

3 pounds chicken parts, preferably bone-in
1 tablespoon Portuguese 5-Spice (see page 37)
1 tablespoon salt
1 (28-ounce) can crushed tomatoes
Water or a mixture of water and chicken broth (about 8 cups, total)
1 large carrot, peeled and diced
1 large potato, peeled and diced
1 cup vermicelli or fine spaghetti, broken into 2- to 3-inch lengths

Rub chicken pieces with 5-Spice and salt. In a large soup pot, combine chicken, tomatoes and water; bring to a boil and simmer 20 minutes. Add carrots, simmer 5 minutes; add potatoes, simmer 10 minutes. Bring to a boil again, add pasta and cook until pasta is al dente. Taste and correct seasonings with pepper, piri piri (page 36) or more 5-Spice as desired.

SPLIT PEA SOUP PORTUGUESE

Makes 6 servings

One definition of eternity is two people and a ham. But from time to time, it is worthwhile to buy a whole, bone-in ham, spend some time processing it and enjoy several excellent meals. Roast ham with pineapple (or use our lemon sauce, page 39). Cut meat from bone and slice for sandwiches or cut into chunks to serve with cheese and olives. Then save that precious bone, with some scraps attached, for this soup, my mom's favorite.

> 1 ham bone
> Water or chicken stock
> 2 tablespoons olive oil
> 1 large onion, chopped
> 1 medium carrot, diced
> 2 ounces raw long-grain rice
> 1 pound split peas, soaked overnight in water, drain well
> 1 teaspoon salt
> 1/4 teaspoon white pepper
> 2/3 cup diced ham
> Homemade croutons*

In a large, heavy-bottomed soup pot, combine ham bone and 8 cups water. Bring to a boil, skim foam and simmer 45 minutes. Meanwhile, in a sauté pan, heat olive oil over medium-high heat and sauté onion and carrot until onion is limp and translucent and carrot beginning to cook and grow golden at the edges. Taste stock and season as desired; remove ham bone and add the onion-carrot mixture, rice and drained split peas with salt and pepper to taste. Bring to a boil, reduce heat to simmer and simmer 30 minutes. Add ham and cook a few minutes until meat is warmed through. Serve topped with homemade croutons.

Variation: For a really creamy, soup, purée in batches before adding ham.

*To make croutons: Preheat oven to 350°F. Using a good compagne (country-style) bread, cut 1-inch squares to equal 1 to 2 cups. Spread on a cookie sheet and bake until crisp, 10 to 15 minutes. Melt together 1 tablespoon each butter and olive oil and place in a large bowl with 1 clove minced garlic. Toss the croutons in the garlic butter, keeping them moving so the flavoring is evenly spread. Cool and store in paper (not plastic) bags.

THE POTATO SOUP FAMILY

Tip: Never "mash" potatoes in a food processor or with an electric mixer; vigorous mixing brings out the starch and creates an unpleasant "glue." Use a ricer or hand-held masher. More work, better texture.

Tip: Some people drizzle ½ cup or so of fruity olive oil into Portuguese-style potato soup at the point when they add the vegetables for flavor and silky texture.

Caldo Verde
GREEN SOUP
Makes 4 to 6 servings

Although ubiquitous in the Portuguese world, caldo verde isn't much seen in Hawai'i. It may have been that Portuguese, rice eaters before they got here, just went with the dominant rice flow. We didn't eat potatoes often in my house, but when we did, it was in stew or with the very occasional beef roast.

Still, potato-based soups are ridiculously easy. This one, often served in mugs and topped with salpicao (a pickled pork sausage unavailable here), hails from Minho in mainland Portugal but is found everywhere Portuguese live. In Portugal, street vendors use special graters to produce grass-thin shreds of couves galega (Portuguese cabbage) to order. At home, julienne the cabbage or collards as thinly as possible, or try the shredding blade of a food processor.

> 4 cups chicken broth (roughly 2 cans)
> 4 cups water
> 4 to 5 large baking potatoes, peeled and cut into chunks
> 1 onion, chopped
> 3 cloves garlic, peeled and mashed
> 1 teaspoon salt
> 2 bunches collard greens or 12 to 15 large Portuguese cabbage leaves

(continued on the next page)

8 to 10 ounces linguiça (Portuguese sausage), chopped into small bits

In a large soup pot, bring broth and water to a boil. Add potatoes, onion, garlic and salt. Lower heat to medium and allow to simmer until potatoes are falling-apart soft. Remove from heat and carefully mash potatoes in broth until smooth (or remove potatoes with slotted spoon and mash in bowl, then return to broth).

While the soup is heating, wash the collards or Portuguese cabbage, stack leaves, roll them into a cigar shape and julienne very thinly. Just before serving, bring the soup to a boil, add the cabbage or collards and linguiça and simmer 5 minutes until greens are bright green and soup is heated through. Serve immediately.

Variations:

- **Watercress Potato-Pea Soup:** Make the Caldo Verde as above with these changes: Add ½ cup dried split peas to boiling broth along with potatoes, onions, garlic and salt. And, instead of collards, wash 1 bunch watercress and chop into 1-inch length, separating the delicate leaves from the tougher stems. Place the stems in the boiling potato soup and simmer 10 minutes; add leaves just prior to serving and heat just until wilted. Serve immediately.

- **Pumpkin Potato Soup:** Instead of collards, add pumpkin chunks to the potato soup. Small Japanese kabocha are easy to use, though hard to cut. To soften, stab 1 kabocha in a couple of places to allow the release of steam. Microwave the whole, unpeeled pumpkin on high 7 to 10 minutes. Wearing oven mitts, remove from microwave and cool until touchable. Cut pumpkin in half, scoop out seeds and strings. Slice into quarters; cut flesh away from pumpkin skin and into bite-size chunks. After mashed potatoes are returned to broth, add pumpkin and bring to a boil, reduce heat and simmer until pumpkin is soft. Serve immediately.

Carnes e Aves

MEATS

Portuguese are inveterate meat-eaters, even though fish and shellfish are more plentiful. Pork is our favorite. Beef, rather scarce in our homeland, is second. Sausage and other aged meats are everyday fare.

PORTUGUESE POT ROAST
Serves 6 to 8

Vinegar- or wine-based marinades are standard in Portuguese cooking, using varied spicing and aromatics. Here, a wide range of highly flavored ingredients infuse a beef roast—boneless rolled roast (a tougher cut pounded flat by the butcher, then rolled and tied with string; order in advance) or chuck roast (seven-bone, blade or eye of chuck), or any cut recommended for braising rather than roasting.

 1 small onion, finely chopped
 3 cloves garlic, minced
 1 cup vinegar
 1½ cups dry white wine or dry sherry
 1 tablespoon Dijon-style mustard, preferably grainy
 1 tablespoon paprika
 1 tablespoon allspice
 4 bay leaves, crumbled
 1 tablespoon Hawaiian honey
 2 teaspoons flaked sea salt
 4 to 5 pound beef roast (suggestions above)
 ¼ pound bacon ends (aka seasoning bacon), chopped
 ¾ cup flour, divided use
 ½ teaspoon salt
 ¼ teaspoon pepper
 6 small peeled baking potatoes or 3 large potatoes, peeled and cut in half
 3 tablespoons butter, softened

In a large, nonreactive bowl or enameled cast iron Dutch oven (such as a Le Crueset), combine onion, garlic, vinegar, wine, mustard, paprika, allspice, bay leaves, honey and salt. Immerse roast in marinade and marinate 6 to 8 hours. Remove roast from marinade and drain on paper towels; wipe dry. Pour marinade into oversize measuring cup. Wipe out pot and lightly brown bacon ends over medium heat. Season ½ cup flour with salt and pepper and dredge the roast in the seasoned flour.

(continued on page 48)

Carnes e Aves

Return roast to pot and brown on all sides. Arrange potatoes around roast. Strain half the marinade into the pot and simmer, covered, 1 to 2 hours, until tender, periodically spooning marinade over if the top of the roast becomes exposed. In a small bowl, make a buerre marnie (butter-flour thickener) by combining remaining ¼ cup flour with softened butter to make a soft paste. Stir some hot marinade into the butter-flour mixture until liquid enough to pour around the beef roast to thicken the gravy. Roast should reach 145 to 150°F on an instant-read thermometer.

PORTUGUESE POT ROAST II

Makes 6 servings

For every Portuguese cook there's a different pot roast recipe. This one typifies the Portuguese love affair with tomato-based sauces.

½ cup olive oil
1 (3-pound) boneless chuck roast , dried with paper towels
3 cloves garlic, mashed
1 whole onion, coarsely chopped
1 bunch flat-leaf parsley, coarsely chopped
1 cup dry red wine (possibly more)
1 teaspoon flaked sea salt
½ teaspoon finely ground black pepper
2 teaspoons Portuguese 5-spice (see page 37)
1 tablespoon walnuts, very finely minced
1 (28-ounce) can crushed tomatoes

Preheat oven to 350°F. In a heavy Dutch oven, heat olive oil until shimmering. Place roast in hot olive oil and brown well on all sides, adjusting heat so that the roast is neither burning nor stewing. Add garlic, onions, parsley, wine, salt, pepper, Portuguese spice, walnuts and crushed tomatoes. Place in 350°F oven and braise, covered, 60 to 90 minutes, checking periodically to see if it needs liquid; if liquid cooks off to less than ½ inch, add another ½ cup of wine. When meat is tender, remove to a rimmed platter, spooning sauce over.

Carnes e Aves

PORTUGUESE STEAK

Serves 4

Portuguese love a good steak, generally rubbed with garlic and served with fresh-made onion sauce spiked with a little tomato.

1 recipe cebolada sauce (onion sauce; page 38)
3 ounces tomato paste
4 (6-ounce) steaks (your choice of cut, but suitable for grilling)
2 to 3 tablespoons olive oil
Sea salt and freshly ground pepper to taste
2 to 3 cloves garlic, finely minced

Make cebolada, stir in tomato paste, cook briefly and set aside—keep warm or allow to come to room temperature.

Wipe and dry steaks (try dry-aging them a bit; wrap in paper towels and refrigerate 24 hours).

Using a mortar and pestle, make a paste of the olive oil, salt, pepper and garlic. Rub steaks well with this paste. Grill to desired doneness, turning once. As with any fried meats or fish, use tongs gently to check for the proper browning, but do not poke, prod or turn steaks repeatedly, which drains moisture

Serve on a bed of sauce, or on a bed of rice or mashed potatoes with sauce poured over.

MADEIRAN KEBABS
Makes 4 to 6 servings

O ne of Madeira's most popular dishes, skewered beef with bay leaf, seems not to have made it to Hawai'i; at least, I've never seen a recipe for it in any local cookbook. It's as though the dominance of Asian-style grilling stamped it out early on. Bay grows well here and fresh bay is available at farmers' markets.

> 2 pounds beef ribe-eye, tenderloin, sirloin or striploin, cut into 1½-inch cubes
> ¼ cup butter, melted
> 4 tablespoons olive oil
> 4 cloves garlic, mashed
> 3 to 5 fresh bay leaves, bruised between your hands
> Sea salt and freshly ground pepper

Place the beef in a large, flat casserole. In a small bowl, mix together butter, olive oil and garlic.

Crumble a handful of bay leaves into small pieces and add to butter mixture. Season to taste with salt and pepper, then place on beef. Cover and marinate several hours. Heat a charcoal grill to white-ash stage or place a gas grill on high. Thread beef chunks on 4 to 6 bay branches or skewers, placing bay leaves between every couple of beef chunks. Grill the kebabs, turning to evenly brown each side, about 4 to 6 minutes for medium rare; do not overcook.

Note on skewers: If you have access to a bay tree, select four to six thin, woody branches and strip off the leaves. Metal or bamboo skewers (soak bamboo in water 15 minutes so they don't burn) may be substituted.

PIQUANT PORTUGUESE CHOPS
Makes 4 servings

B ecause grazing land was scarce in the Atlantic Islands, pigs and chicken were the favored land animals. In the days before farmers bred the fat out of the pig, we used to have pork chops often, in this simple way. Fortunately, we are once again seeing tender cuts of pork in stores (look for locally grown pork).

- 1 tablespoon light olive oil
- 4 center-cut, thick-sliced pork chops, preferably local kuro-buta (black Berkshire pig)
- 1 large, sweet Maui onion (or two small)
- 2 cloves garlic, mashed
- ¼ cup cider vinegar
- 1 teaspoon flaked sea salt
- 1 tablespoon honey
- 1 tablespoon white wine

Heat olive oil and fry pork chops quickly until golden-brown turning once. Remove pork chops from oil to heat-proof casserole; cover and place in 200°F oven. Peel, halve, cut onion into slivers; peel and mince garlic and sweat together in oil over medium heat. Add cider vinegar, salt, honey and white wine. Cook three minutes, scraping up dark bits and mixing in pan juices. Remove pork chops, cover with onions and drizzle onion sauce over meat.

Tip: The USDA has lowered the suggested internal cooking temperature for pork to match that of beef or chicken: 145°F.

THE PIG MAN: ALVIN JARDINE

Alvin Jardine's business card is a creased turquois rectangle that shows a heavily tusked wild boar. The name on it is "The Pig Man."

Some years ago, Jardine, who lives in Mountain View, drove to Hāmākua Springs Country Farm to give visiting chef Alan Wong and his staff (and tag-along me) a lesson in smoking meat.

As do many older hunters no longer hardy enough to engage in a day of hunting, he trades his skill as a smoke chef for a share of friends' hunting largesse. He smokes hundreds of pounds a year: wild boar, but also domestic pork and commercial beef, pork sausage, fish, even mutton.

His smoker is a metal shed raised off the ground on cement blocks, allowing free air flow to the ʻohiʻa and ironwood fire below. A metal cap shields the fire from contact with fat that drips from the meat. Metal rods suspended between the walls of the shed hold ropes of pipikaula and shoyu-marinated pork. Long coils of Portuguese-style sausage are twined around sticks of hard, strong strawberry guava wood.

While the meat smoked, Jardine talked story. His helpers had been using a commercial sausage stuffer. But, he said, "In the olden days, we used a cow horn jus' like a funnel, eh? You push 'em through with a stick and you make a little groove in the horn where you can tie the casing on. Work good."

Jardin helps to "seed" his own smoking material through the practice called lahoʻole—catching a young wild pig and castrating it, then releasing it back into the wild. "When you castrate a boar, they don't travel with the herd, they don't go too far, they get more fat, the meat is not so tough. That's the best for sausage."

He recalled that at one time, pipikaula—Hawaiian-style jerky—was just beef and salt; today, shoyu and other marinade ingredients are used. In the past, cowboys would skin and gut the beef, chop it up, bones and all, and layer the meat in a crock with salt, brining it for 15 days. The meat would then be well washed and layered with salt again. "Ho, da t'ing last forevah!"

Smoking was another way to extend shelf life, said Jardine, who began hunting when he was just 7 or 8 years old, with his grandfather, a mountain man whose job was finding water for the plantations, and who often spent a month at a time in the hills.

Before he smokes meat, he brines it. For a plastic tub the size of a laundry basket, Jardine uses four gallons of water and adds Hawaiian salt to taste (he literally tastes the water; it should be salty but not off-puttingly so). If he's smoking wild game, he adds a cup of baking soda to reduce the gamey flavor. The meat marinates for an hour, then it's rinsed and immersed again in a flavoring marinade. If the meat is tough—wild boar or range-raised beef—he'll add one peeled, mashed green papaya as a tenderizer. The marinade might be red wine, garlic and lots of chili pepper for pipikaula, or shoyu, sugar, Hawaiian salt and lots of garlic for smoked pork. Some people flavor the sausage with paprika, lots and lots of garlic, chilies and Hawaiian salt.

The 100 pounds of meat that Jardine and friends prepared for the Wong party took four hours to smoke.

Jardine absolutely loves "smoke meat"—with red beans and rice, in Portuguese bean soup, fried with soy beans for pūpū, in scrambled eggs or just sliced, fried and scattered over hot, steamed rice. "Ho! No can beat 'em."

Pig hunter Al Jardine (right) is aided in preparing sausage for smoking by Kimo Pa of Hāmākua Springs Farm.

(Note: Alvin Jardine died in 2014. Though he was too ill or shy to talk with me for this book, I have never forgotten our day smoking meat at Hāmākua Springs Country Farm (now, alas!, also gone).)

POT ROAST PORK WITH LEMON SAUCE
Makes 6 to 8 servings

The Hawaiian Islands, like the Portuguese Atlantic Islands, once were home to dozens of varieties of citrus. That, combined with the Portuguese taste for piquant flavors, means many dishes feature lemon and orange. Meyer lemons, with their lovely acid-sweet balance, are particularly nice.

> 1 (3-pound) pork butt, rib or blade roast
> 3 cloves garlic, finely minced
> 1 tablespoon fresh thyme leaves
> ½ teaspoon salt
> ¼ teaspoon finely ground black pepper
> Zest and juice of 2 lemons
> 2 additional lemons, finely sliced
> ½ onion, minced
> 1 stalk celery, minced
> 1 recipe lemon sauce (see page 39)

Wipe pork roast with paper towels. Rub pork roast with garlic, thyme salt, pepper and zest and place in a zippered plastic bag. Combine juice of 2 lemons (about ¼ cup) with equal amount of water and pour over pork roast. Marinate 1 hour.

Preheat oven to 325°F. Place roast on rack in oven roasting pan. Arrange thinly sliced lemons over pork roast and sprinkle onions and celery over roast. Pour ½ inch water in the bottom of the roasting pan to collect the juices and release moisture during roasting. Roast 3 to 4 hours, to 145°F internal temperature. Remove from oven, cover loosely with foil tent and allow to rest 10 to 15 minutes. Prepare the lemon sauce, adding some of the lemon water from the roasting pan, with scraped-up solids. Serve sauce drizzled over sliced roast.

Variation: Instead of a roast, use thick-cut kurobuta pork chops, marinate as above; dry well and fry in vegetable oil or bacon drippings. Serve drizzled with lemon sauce.

GRANDMA'S PORK CHOPS RICE

Makes 4 servings as a one-dish meal

A friend reminded me of this dish, one that her mother, as well as mine, made often, when pork chops were actually inexpensive.

2 cups long-grain white rice
4 cups chicken or pork broth (preferably homemade; see
   recipe on page 62)
4 thin pork chops
1 teaspoon salt
¼ teaspoon pepper
Minced garlic, about 2 to 4 cloves
Olive oil
1 very thinly sliced onion

In a wide, high, heavy-bottomed pan such as a well-seasoned cast iron pan, a Dutch oven or a nonstick high-rimmed frying pan, place the rice and broth. Bring to a boil. Meanwhile rub pork chops with salt, pepper and garlic. In a sauté pan, fry pork chops very briefly in hot olive oil, just to golden-brown; reduce heat to medium-low. Sprinkle onion over boiling rice and water. Arrange pork chops on top. Cover and simmer about 15 minutes until rice is tender and pork chops are cooked to 145°F on an instant-read thermometer.

Carnes e Aves

BLOOD SAUSAGE
Makes about 2 pounds sausage

Every year, my great-uncle, Manuel Duarte, who had a pig farm just down the road from Grandpa's house, would kill a few pigs. His wife, Auntie Margaret, would make her famous blood sausage. Those sensitive about the name, not to mention the midnight color, would not partake, but they were missing something good—rich, a little spicy, full-flavored. You can buy pig's blood in some Filipino markets. I love this lightly fried, with eggs scrambled in.

2 tablespoons vegetable oil
4 cloves garlic, mashed and minced
1 small yellow onion, finely chopped
2 pounds well-marbled pork, or fatty ground pork, chopped
3 small, hot red Hawaiian chili peppers (niʻoi)
1 tablespoon Hawaiian salt
4 to 5 cups green onion (1/4-inch lengths), chopped
1 1/2 teaspoons ground cinnamon
1/2 teaspoon ground allspice
1/8 teaspoon ground cloves
1/4 teaspoon ground black pepper
1/2 teaspoon ground nutmeg
1/2 teaspoon ground cumin
1 pound pig's blood

In a deep, heavy bottomed Dutch oven, heat oil and fry garlic and onion until wilted and golden. Add pork and fry until meat is no longer pink. Stir in remaining ingredients, except blood, and simmer 10 to 15 minutes. Add blood, mix well and cook 15 to 20 minutes, stirring from time to time. Cool and form into patties or fill sausage casings.

A WAIALUA FAMILY

The late Cecilia Vincent De Coito Guerreiro was born in Waialua, Oʻahu, the eleventh of twelve children of first-generation Portuguese parents, Antone Vincent De Coito and Maria Teixeira Correa. Some years ago, Cecilia sat down with me and her youngest daughter, Gina Loveland, with whom she lived in Wahiawā Heights.

Theirs was an important family in the Portuguese neighborhood of Waialua Plantation's Mill Camp: Cecilia's grandmother was the parteira, the midwife, and her mother was the amamentara, a wet nurse. It was her father's

Cecilia Vincent De Coito Guerreiro (approximately 19 years old)

job, among others, to go into the territorial offices to register camp births occurred. Ironically, he neglected to record Cecilia's.

In other words, she said gaily, "I was never born." Later, she would have to rely on school records as proof of citizenship.

Though she acknowledged that the daily work in a mill camp was rigorous and never-ending, Cecilia spoke of her young life with fondness.

Her father nurtured a large garden, raising potatoes, cabbage, string beans, lettuce and the Portuguese cabbage they called "kale." There was a tiny orchard, too, with oranges, grapes for wine and peaches—"Oh, those peaches! Sooo sweet."

And, as in every Portuguese yard, a lemon tree gave juice, not only for cooking, but for sanitizing and sweetening the hands. The family had chickens and bought fish from passing vendors. Pork came from a periodic communal pig-killing at a farm in nearby Kamaloa. These gatherings were quite an operation, with her father supervising the butchering and her mother in charge of carefully storing and husbanding the family's portion of the pork.

The pig-killing was the work of several days. Lard had to be rendered, intestines stripped, washed and salvaged for casings. The various cuts of meat were carved by the men. The trimmings were chopped and mixed with garlic and spices to make chourice (a spicy sausage) and, more familiar today, linguiça (sweeter, more garlickey), which would then be smoked: hung from the rafters in a closed shed where a dampened fire produced a slow smoke. The blood became blood sausage.

"There would be competitions between the families to see who made the best," Cecilia recalled.

Cecilia recalled vividly how her father would layer various cuts of raw pork with solid fat in the kelemania, as large crocks of German make were called in adapted Hawaiian. The crocks, which once contained pickles, sauerkraut or other German products, were begged, bought or bartered for, and every house had a collection of various sizes.

"Everything had to be done under Mama's eye. You had to be clean, clean," said Cecilia, who would put her mother up against a modern-day surgeon for the thoroughness of her hand-washing, right up to the arms until the skin was flushed and almost painful.

In the Vincent De Coito household, one crock held pork and the other homemade wine. Her father grew both red and white grapes in an arbor over the chicken coop. Papa would taste them daily, determining when they had reached the proper brix (measure of sugar). Mama was in charge of aging the wine.

"Mama would take a clean cloth and strain the juice through it," Cecilia recalled. "You would wring it out to get as much as you could,

Cecilia (approximately 19 years old)

put a little sugar, a clean cloth over, and keep it in the pantry. Mama would check it every day." When she and Papa judged the wine ready, he would invite "the old Portuguese men" over to taste the new vintage while playing a round of bisca, a card game. One can imagine their readiness to help with this task. The finished wine was also a daily beverage for the family: "just a small glass at dinnertime," Cecilia said. "but everyone got one who was old enough to hold a glass."

Altogether, said Cecilia, "a good life."

(Note: Cecilia Vincent De Coito Guerreiro died in 2002.)

Linguiça Pica
SPICY PORTUGUESE SAUSAGE
Make 4 pounds sausage

I n 2011, my friend David Izumi, a master smoker, taught a sausage-making session at our church. It was actually a friendly competition in which a half-dozen people (few of them Portuguese) attempted to make linguiça with recipes of their own creation. My sausage was delicious—spicy and exotic, but it wasn't linguiça. Later, I worked on the recipe; here's my revised version.

To make stuffed sausage, you need specialized equipment and hard-to-find pork casings. Having helped stuff 20 pounds of sausage, our entire group decided sausage patties were just fine. Even 4 pounds is a lot: Make this with friends or family.

4 pounds well-marbled boneless pork butt with surface fat
15 cloves garlic, minced or pressed
6 to 12 small, hot Hawaiian chili peppers, minced
4 to 6 tablespoons Portuguese 5-spice (see Temperos e Salsas, page 37)
2 tablespoons ground cumin
½ cup paprika
2 tablespoons salt
1 tablespoon freshly ground pepper
½ cup sugar
3 drops Liquid Smoke
½ cup vinegar
½ cup dry red wine
¼ teaspoon red food coloring mixed with 2 tablespoons water

Cut pork into cubes. Grind coarsely. If you lack a meat grinder, mince the meat very fine (you can use the Chinese method of chopping simultaneously with two cleavers; it really works). Do not use a food processor; the meat will become a paste.

In a large bowl, combine meat with remaining ingredients and mix well. The best tool for this is your hands; wear kitchen gloves if prefer.

Heat a little vegetable oil in a frying pan; pinch off enough pork mixture to make a small patty; fry and taste. Correct seasonings.

Cover tightly and refrigerate overnight to allow flavors to blend and mellow. Shape into patties and refrigerate up to one week, or freeze, with squares of kitchen parchment between the patties. Of, if you're ambitious, fill pork casings, smoke and refrigerate or freeze to preserve.

PORK WITH PAPAYA AND PUMPKIN
Makes 6 servings

If you hunt, or are given a gift of boar meat, try this typically Portuguese stew using a dry sherry or red wine vinegar marinade. The idea came to me when I was talking to Cecilia Vincente-DeCoito Guerreiro (profiled on page 58); she mentioned that her mother often used green papaya in beef and pork stews because the papain enzyme in the fruit tenderized the meat. Al Jardine (profiled on page 92), does the same.

    2 to 3 cloves garlic, sliced
    1 sweet or red onion, finely sliced
    1 celery stalk, finely sliced
    4 to 5 green onions, finely sliced
    1 cup dry amontillado sherry
    ½ cup red wine vinegar
    1 tablespoon brown sugar, honey, agave syrup
    ½ teaspoon salt
    1 large fresh bay leaf, crumbled into small pieces
    2 pounds pork butt or wild boar roast
    1 tablespoon olive oil
    4 slices center-cut bacon, finely chopped
    1 (8-ounce) can tomato sauce
    1 cinnamon stick

(continued on the next page)

1½ to 2 cups pork or beef stock
2 kabocha pumpkins
3 unripe papaya or green cooking papaya (Filipino or Thai markets)
Olive oil

In a large, nonreactive bowl or other container, combine garlic, onion, celery, green onion, sherry, vinegar, sweetener, salt, bay leaf and meat. Marinate, turning periodically, at least 4 hours (for pork) or as long as overnight (a must for wild, gamey-flavored meats).

Preheat oven to 350°F.

Drain roast, reserving marinade, and pat dry. In a large, heavy-bottomed Dutch oven, fry bacon until lightly browned but still a bit limp; drain on paper towels and reserve; wipe out pot. In the same pot, heat 1 tablespoon olive oil over medium-high heat. Brown roast on all sides. Add drained bacon, tomato sauce, cinnamon stick, stock and reserved marinade with vegetables. Roast should be almost completely covered by liquid.

Cook in 350°F oven for 1 to 2 hours, spooning liquid over meat occasionally, until meat is fork-tender and liquid reduced.

Meanwhile, pierce kabocha pumpkin with knife in one or two places; microwave on high for 7 to 10. Cool. Halve kabocha and remove seeds and strings. With a short, thing-bladed knife, carve flesh away from skin, losing as little flesh as possible. Cut flesh into chunks (about 1½ inches on a side). Cut away papaya stem, cut papaya in half; remove seeds and strings, cut flesh from skin and cut flesh into chunks.

Twenty minutes or so before the stew is done, stir papaya and pumpkin into pork roast liquid surrounding roast. If the roast liquid is too thin and soupy, make a slurry of 1 tablespoon cornstarch to 1 tablespoon cooking liquid, whisked, and stir into pot. Allow to cook a bit longer to thicken.

Remove pot from oven and remove cinnamon stick. Remove meat from gravy, slice as desired and top with vegetables, papaya, pumpkin and gravy.

Galinha Portugueza
PORTUGUESE CHICKEN
Makes 6 servings

hicken most often went into soup in our house, though we had the occasional roast chicken. The treatments are usually very simple. Here's a recipe a cousin gave me.

Vegetable oil for deep-frying
6 large, skin-on, bone-in chicken thighs
Flour seasoned with 1 teaspoon salt and ½ teaspoon pepper for dredging
12 ounces Portuguese sausage
1 stalk celery, stringed and cut into strips
1 red or yellow bell pepper, cut into strips
1 (28-ounce) can chopped tomatoes (or an equal volume of fresh, very ripe chopped heirloom tomatoes)
3 ounces (half a can) tomato paste
1 cup water
1 bunch flat-leaf parsley, chopped

Preheat oven to 325°F. Place 2 inches oil in a deep, heavy-bottomed pot such as a Dutch oven and heat to 350°F. Dredge the chicken thighs evenly in seasoned flour and deep-fry (don't crowd them, work in batches) until golden; no need to cook through as this is the first of a two-stage cooking process.

Set chicken aside and pour off all but 1 tablespoon oil. Heat this oil and brown sausage, bell pepper and celery; remove sausage and vegetables from heat; reserve. Place tomatoes, tomato sauce, water and parsley in the drippings. Boil and reduce by one-third. Add chicken and vegetables.

Bake at 325°F for 30 minutes. Arrange and serve on platter.

CHICKEN WITH OLIVES
Makes 6 servings

This simple dish is home cookin' for a Portuguese. Marjoram, though not much used now, was popular with Portuguese both on the mainland and in the Atlantic Isles, found in many gardens. Although Portuguese prefer plain green olives, these can be hard to find; Spanish olives are fine, but a mix of Spanish and kalamata lends the dish a piquant saltiness.

1 tablespoon rendered bacon fat or lard
2 whole yellow onions, peeled and chopped
1 whole chicken, sectioned*
Flaked sea salt and freshly ground black pepper
2 teaspoons dried marjoram
1 cup chicken stock (more, if needed)
½ bunch flat-leaf parsley, finely chopped
1 cup seeded green olives, Spanish olives, halved or 1 cup
  seeded kalamata olives or a mixture

In a deep skillet or heavy-bottomed Dutch oven, melt fat or lard over medium heat and gently caramelize onions until golden. Rub chicken pieces well with salt, pepper and dried marjoram.

Place chicken in fat and brown on both sides just until golden (not crispy brown). Pour stock over chicken, cover and cook 20 minutes. Sprinkle parsley and olives over chicken, add more stock if needed, cover and cook until chicken is cooked through (145°F on instant-read cooking thermometer). Serve hot with rice or steamed or fried pumpkin.

* Section raw chicken at joints and along bone lines so that you have wings, drumsticks, breasts cut in half. Or use pre-cut bone-in chicken pieces, such as two halved breasts and four thighs.

Tip: Though it's not necessarily a Portuguese tradition, brining poultry before roasting somehow unscrambles the protein infrastructure of the meat so that it doesn't tighten and dry out. Thus, a high-heat method can be used to produce crisp skin without drying out the chicken breast.

CHICKEN WITH APRICOTS
Makes 4 to 6 servings

Fruit and meats are much more common in European cooking than they are in the U.S. Here's a Portuguese idea.

8 ounces dried apricots, cut into strips*
1 tablespoon butter
1 tablespoon olive oil
6 skin-on, boned chicken thighs
1 small yellow onion, chopped
3 cloves garlic, chopped
1 teaspoon Portuguese 5-Spice (see page 37)
1 cup dry white wine (preferably Portuguese vinho verde)
1/4 cup red wine vinegar (more, if needed for balance)
2 tablespoons honey
1/2 cup fruit juice (apricot nectar, pear nectar, apple juice, white cranberry juice)
1/2 teaspoon salt
1/4 teaspoon pepper

Soak apricots, if needed (see below); drain and place on paper towels. In a heavy-bottomed Dutch oven over medium-high heat, melt together butter and olive oil. Place chicken pieces, skin side-down, in pan and brown well, about 3 to 5 minutes per side. Remove chicken to a plate and reserve.

In remaining butter and oil, over medium heat, gently saute onion, garlic and Portuguese 5-Spice until onions are limp and translucent. Sprinkle half the apricots in the frying pan, return the chicken to the pot.

In a bowl or oversize measuring cup, whisk together wine, vinegar, honey and fruit juice. Pour over chicken. Sprinkle remaining apricots over chicken. Cover and braise over medium to medium-low heat on the stovetop until chicken is cooked through, about 20 minutes.

(continued on page 68)

Taste, season with salt and pepper; taste and correct seasonings with additional wine, vinegar, honey or fruit juice, as needed. Serve hot with Portuguese rice or mashed or fried potatoes.

* If apricots are dry and hard, soak them in a little warm water for 20 minutes. Soft-dried apricots do not need presoaking.

POT ROAST CHICKEN
Makes 4 to 6 servings

This is an easier version of the same recipe, with a slightly different flavor profile. Two wines marry with chicken juices and tomatoes to make a sauce. Use a Portuguese vinho verde; this everyday table wine is quite inexpensive, less than $10 a bottle at fine wine shops in Honolulu.

3 pounds skin-on, bone-in chicken thighs
1 tablespoon olive oil
1 tablespoon butter
1 (14.5-ounce) can chopped tomatoes, with juice
3 cloves garlic, crushed
¼ cup flat-leaf parsley, chopped
½ cup dry sherry or dry white wine (such as a Portuguese vinho verde)
½ cup Madeira wine
1 teaspoon salt
¼ teaspoon pepper

Preheat oven to 350°F. In the bottom of a heavy-bottomed pot or Dutch oven with an oven-proof lid, heat together olive oil and butter over medium-high heat. Brown chicken thighs just until golden, turning once. Add remaining ingredients, cover and bake at 350°F 1 hour. Remove cover and bake 15 minutes to crisp and brown chicken.

Variation: Add 1 cup halved Spanish olives along with tomatoes and wine.

PORTUGUESE FRIED CHICKEN
Makes 4 to 6 servings

The Portuguese technique with fried chicken is exactly that of the Japanese: The chicken is first marinated, then breaded and fried (Japanese use panko and Portuguese a flour coating).

3 pounds boned chicken thighs
1 recipe vinha d'ahlos marinade (page 41)
1 cup flour
½ teaspoon salt
¼ teaspoon pepper
½ teaspoon red pepper flakes, crushed
Vegetable oil for frying

In a nonreactive bowl, marinate chicken thighs in vinha d'ahlos mixture, covered, overnight in the refrigerator. Drain well and pat dry. In a bowl, combine flour, salt and pepper to taste and red pepper flakes; whisk to combine. Dredge chicken in flour mixture.

Preheat oven to warm, 150°F. In a large, heavy, open pot, heat 1½ inch of oil to 350°F. Place chicken in hot fat and fry to golden brown, turning once. Internal temperature should be 155°F on an instant-read thermometer. Don't crowd chicken; work in batches. Keep each batch warm in oven, draining on paper towels, until all chicken is done.

ROSEMARY CHICKEN
Makes 6 to 8 servings

Alecrim (ah-lay-CRING), rosemary, is much prized by Portuguese not just for its culinary properties but for its ability, they say, to ward off the evil eye. It is considered sacred to the Blessed Mother. My Portuguese teacher taught me a song listing the attributes of a true Portuguese home, with a bush of rosemary in the front courtyard a central feature. Use fresh rosemary (it grows very well in Hawai'i, even in pots) for brining and stuffing, but powdered for seasoning the skin. Chomping into a full leaf of rosemary overwhelms the palate and isn't pleasant.

One 5 to 6 pound whole roasting chicken, washed in cold water

For the brine:
1 gallon cold water
3/4 cup Hawaiian salt*
3/4 cup sugar
1/4 cup olive oil
2 to 3 fresh sprigs rosemary

For roasting:
Flaked sea salt and freshly ground black pepper
Dash powdered, dried rosemary (optional)
Olive oil for glazing chicken
1 onion, chopped
1 tart cooking apple, unpeeled, chopped
2 to 3 sprigs fresh rosemary

(continued on the next page)

Four or five hours before serving: Prepare brine in a nonreactive non-stick soup pot, plastic tub, Styrofoam cooler, insulated cooler bag or other container large enough to accommodate water and chicken. Combine cold water, Hawaiian salt, sugar, olive oil and 2 to 3 sprigs rosemary, broken and rubbed well in your hands before dropping into brine. Brine chicken 2 hours.

Preheat oven to 425°F. Remove chicken from brine, rinse well, pat dry. Place some salt and pepper and a dash of powdered rosemary in a small bowl, drizzle in a little olive oil and work to a paste. Rub chicken with this paste inside and out. Place onion, apple and remaining fresh rosemary sprigs inside chicken. With cotton kitchen string, truss the legs of the chicken together. Cut a slit in the skin on either side and tuck the wing tips under the skin. Place on an oven rack and roast 90 minutes.

Chicken is done when it's a caramel-brown, juices run clear when thighs are pierced and internal temperature at thickest part of thigh is 160°F. Tent chicken with foil and allow to rest 10 minutes.

*To dissolve salt, mix with a little hot water and stir well.

Cozido Autentico
BOILED DINNER
Makes 6 servings

Grandma periodically made a "boiled dinner" heavily influenced by Yankee ideas. It was steamed, not boiled, on a rack in the oven, and consisted of corned beef, potatoes, cabbage and carrots. Delicious, but it wasn't a true cozido—a slow-cooked multi-meat boiled dinner served in two or three courses.

The first time I made cozido, we were vacationing on a friend's property. The man in the next house still talks about the smells pouring out our door. We shared the meal with him and he now calls me his "kitchen muse." That kind of reception makes the work worth it.

2 pounds well-marbled pork roast, in large chunks
2 pounds beef chuck roast, in large chunks
1 ham hock
Water to cover meat in a large soup pot
1 bunch parsley, washed, left whole and tied with cotton
   string
1 onion, quartered
2 pounds skin-on, bone-in chicken thighs
1 teaspoon EACH salt and white pepper
1 teaspoon Portuguese 5-Spice (page 37)
3 potatoes, peeled and quartered
3 carrots, peeled and thick-cut
12 ounces Portuguese sausage
1 bunch Portuguese cabbage, collard greens or baby kale,
   chiffonade (narrow strips)
½ bunch parsley, minced

(continued on the next page)

Place pork roast, chuck roast and ham hock in a heavy-bottomed soup kettle with water to cover. Bring to a boil; skim; add parsley stems and onion. Simmer very gently over medium-low three hours. Remove meats; discard ham hock (or freeze for further use). Reserve beef and pork. Strain solids from broth and discard solids; return broth to stove.

Place pork, beef and chicken in broth along with carrots. Bring to a gentle boil and simmer on medium-low 20 minutes. Add potatoes and sausage; simmer 20 minutes. Add cabbage, collards or kale and cook briefly, just until bright green and still slightly crisp.

Using a slotted spoon, carefully scoop out meats and vegetables, arranging them in an attractive heat-proof casserole with a cover. Place in a warm oven.

Ladle broth into six warmed open, shallow bowls. Serve this broth as a first course with bread, croutons or bread rounds that have been sprinkled with a little sharp, dry cheese before toasting. Remove meat and vegetables from the oven, slice and arrange on plates. Garnish with parsley. Serve as a main course. Next day, if there are leftovers, make a third meal: slice or roughly chop remaining meats and vegetables, add water or stock to leftover broth and serve as a thick soup.

Variations:

- Add ½ cup long-grain white rice to the broth after you've removed the meats and vegetables, bring to a boil and cook over medium heat 15 minutes, until rice is cooked through. Serve as first course.

- Soak 2 cups dried garbanzos in water overnight or use canned. Drain and place in broth, along with a bay leaf, to cook after you've removed the meats and vegetables. Bring to a boil and simmer gently until garbanzos are soft. Remove bay leaf. Serve as a first course instead of the plain broth or rice soup.

- Make cozido in slow cooker.

Cozido II
QUICK BOILED DINNER

This is more along the lines of what Grandma used to make and what you'll find in community cookbooks.

Water or chicken broth*
1 corned beef (vacuum-packed, with spices, from grocery store)**
1 medium cabbage***
4 medium potatoes, peeled
2 carrots, peeled, cut into 3-inch lengths
2 cloves garlic, crushed
1 bay leaf, crushed and broken up
Salt and pepper to taste
6 to 8 leaves Portuguese cabbage, collards or kale, washed
Piri piri or vinegar or minced parsley for garnish

In a large pot, such as a Dutch oven, or even a wok, arrange a rack and pour in enough water or chicken broth to rise to just below the rack. Arrange meat, vegetables, and aromatics on rack. Cover and steam over simmering water until meat is tender and vegetables are cooked and flavors have blended, about 30 to 40 minutes. Serve hot, drizzled with piri piri or parsley.

* If you use chicken broth, the juices will melt into the broth and it can be served as a clear soup first course, with the meats and vegetables to follow.

** Some recipes use Portuguese sausage, about 20 ounces (2 lengths or one whole ring), cut into 2-inch lengths. Some use fresh, homemade corned beef, but never canned.

*** Some recipes use Portuguese cabbage (couves) or collards; stack leaves, roll into a cigar shape, cut crosswise into julienne and scatter strips over cozido during the last 5 minutes of cooking. Kale is similarly prepared, but should cook 10 to 15 minutes.

Peixes, Mariscos e Mollusca

FISH, SHELLFISH, MOLLUSKS

For Madeiran and Azorean Portuguese, except those who lived high in the mountains, fish and seafood were an almost everyday food: sardines, mackerel, tuna, but none so popular as salt cod (see Aperetivos).

In Hawai'i, the new islanders' menu of fish dishes seems to have been limited and largely unrecorded. We know they bartered with fishermen neighbors—bread for fresh catch—and continued to enjoy octopus, 'ahi, small fish that resembled sardines, 'opihi, pipipi and abalone. But recipes that survived tend to employ canned or salted fish, with the exception of inexpensive aku (skipjack tuna).

A favorite fish preparation, especially as a snack for parties or family gatherings, was vinha d'ahlos fish: chunks of fish or small whole fish, marinated an hour or two in a vinegar marinade (see Temperos e Salsas), then dusted with flour and quickly fried in lard, bacon fat, olive oil or vegetable oil. It's served hot with toothpicks.

Some people even make a form of vinha d'ahlos poke: Chunks of sashimi-fresh fish are soaked in ice water for a couple of hours, drained, immersed in vinha d'ahlos marinade and refrigerated up to three days, then served, often with an onion dip.

BACALHAO STEW
Makes 4 servings

Bacalhao stew was one of Grandma's fallback recipes and it's easy: Just make a refogado, a tomato stew base, thin it with a flavorful broth (or even wine!) and add some salt cod. We always ate it over rice, of course, though Portuguese would serve it with white bread or broa (yeasted cornbread, page 166).

1 recipe refogado (tomato base, page 71)
6 ounces bacalhao, prepared (see Cod Know-How, page 114)
1 bottle clam juice or equivalent fish stock or white wine
Minced parsley for garnish

Make refogado, thin with clam juice, stock or wine, add codfish and simmer gently to heat through. Serve garnished with parsley, with rice or bread.

"I remember distinctly that we used to sell a lot of codfish, dried codfish, bacalhao, because there were many Portuguese living in Kona. ... It came from the mainland in big sacks and was very dry. If somebody wanted to buy half, we took a saw and cut half. The Portuguese would come down on Sundays—I think it was a tradition in the old country, and many of them wore white suits."

— *Shopkeeper Thomas Kam, speaking of the 1930s and '40s, in the oral history "Traditonal Food Establishments on the Island of Hawai'i" by Nancy Piianaia*

THE PORTUGUESE SAIL TO HAWAI'I

Newcomers are always puzzled by the presence of Portuguese in the islands. Asians, they understand: Hawai'i shares an ocean with Asia. But Portuguese? Aren't we from a continent and an ocean away?

In fact, there has barely been a time in post-contact history when Portuguese were not here. They were mariners who, from the 1400s on, ventured across the globe. "And," wrote Portugal's most revered poet, Luis Vaz de Camoes, "if there had been more of the world, they would have reached it."

Portuguese sailors were among the first to jump ship in Hawai'i in the 1700s. Kamehameha I had a Portuguese secretary, Joao Elliot d'Castro. A handful of Portuguese merchants were well established here the mid-1800s. One of these, Jacintho Perreira, was among the first to recommend Portugal as a source of labor.

In Hawai'i, plantation owners needed workers. In Portugal, meanwhile, the situation was dire. The famed vineyards of Madeira and the Azores were infested with phylloxera, an aphid that stunted or killed grape vines, and the population was decimated by cholera. People were desperate for work, or a way out.

Then came Dr. William Hillebrand, who had lived in Hawai'i, returned to his native Germany and then, stricken with illness, was sent to recover in Madeira's more salubrious climate. He was struck by the similarities between his beloved Hawai'i and these islands, which are much closer to steamy Africa than mainland Europe. The temperature range is 100°F in summer to 44 in winter, but, for the most part, their weather report reads like ours: "Highs in the low 80s, windward showers at higher elevations."

William Hillebrand

Hillebrand wrote to friends in the Hawaiian government, praising the Portuguese Atlantic islanders as "sober, honest, industrious and peaceable." Some spoke a smattering of English. At least, unlike Asians, they shared an alphabet with Caucasians; it was likely they would rapidly become acculturated. Hillebrand was named commissioner of immigration for Hawai'i in 1871 and, after much wrangling between the governments of Portugal and Hawai'i, the first contract laborers boarded the ship *Priscilla* in 1878.

I have the contract of my maternal great-grandfather Arcenio Henriques da Sylva, No. 2519, signed in 1883 by Hillebrand himself, and written in both Portuguese and English. Though he had been trained as both a carpenter and a mason, Great-grandpa, then 36, was to be a simple trabalhador, a laborer, for the princely sum of $9 a month plus a place to live, foodstuffs, medical care and transport to the islands. In return, he pledged three years of his life.

Great-granfather Arcenio Henriques da Sylva's 1883 labor contract.

My young great-aunt Maria, 10, and great-uncle Jose, 8, who traveled with him, would receive a few dollars less. My great-grandmother, pregnant and still tending toddlers, remained behind until he called for her. Together, they would have 10 children, the last two, including my grandmother, born here.

When I was a girl, Grandpa John Gomes Duarte used to tell me that the Portuguese were the most important culture in the world. "We were the kings of the seas," he would declare.

Portuguese in general, and Grandpa in particular, delight in hyperbole, so I paid little attention. But then I minored in history in college and learned about characters such as Henry the Navigator and Vasco Da Gama. Although Portuguese influence had greatly declined by Grandpa's time, he must have been raised on stories of those glory years.

Like so many others, we came here in desperation and stayed in contentment, adding our own threads to the fabric of island life.

COD KNOW-HOW

The salt cod of today is not the cod of your grandparents; it is more lightly salted and needs less processing. Grandma's generation boiled their bacalhao to shreds. In Hawai'i, much of the salt cod goes to the Korean market for making spicy, chewy taegu; it's cheaper but often not as carefully cleaned or boned as the boxed North Atlantic product.

I've had the best luck finding boxed soft-salted North Atlantic cod at Safeway and other large groceries; sometimes fish shops have it.

Here's all you need to do with the boxed product:

- Soak the cod in cold water overnight, draining and refreshing the water at least once.

- Drain and place the cod in fresh cold water in a shallow frying pan or the bottom of a soup pot. Bring the cod just to a boil, immediately turn off heat and allow to steep until cool. Drain well.

- With your fingers, pull flakes apart and pick over to remove any bones and whitish skin. Use as desired.

- There is no need to change the water four or five times or to boil for hours, no matter what your grandmother's recipe book says.

PORTUGUESE/HAWAIIAN COD SALAD

Makes 4 to 6 servings as pūpū or entrée

S ometimes called Cod Salad, this dish is known in many cultures: Spain, Cuba, Puerto Rico and elsewhere. This recipe was sent to me at The Honolulu Advertiser by Margaret K. Grace in 2005. She gave no proportions, but I've made estimates. In some versions, the dish is garnished with slices of hard-boiled egg. And it may be served on a bed of bitter greens for a more sophisticated flavor combination and presentation. Marge loves this with poi. We always had it with freshly cooked rice. Some people like it on bread for open-face sandwiches.

> Vegetable oil for frying
> 1 pound salt cod, prepared, cleaned, flaked (see page 114 for technique)
> 1 sweet onion, thinly sliced and broken into crescents
> 3 to 4 small, red, white or yellow salad potatoes, quartered lengthwise, peeled in strips
> 2 to 4 cloves garlic, peeled and minced
> 3 to 4 stalks green onion, sliced ¼-inch
> 1 to 2 cups fresh, ripe tomatoes, chopped; or equivalent halved cherry or grape tomatoes
> White or cider vinegar as desired
> Salt and pepper to taste

In a large sauté pan, heat vegetable oil over medium heat and fry codfish until slightly golden. Add onions and fry gently a couple of minutes, then add potatoes and garlic and fry until potatoes are a little browned at the edges, onion is golden and translucent. Add green onion and tomatoes. Turn off heat and sprinkle sparingly with vinegar. Season with salt and pepper.

Piexe Frito
FRIED FISH
Makes 4 servings

The classic Island-style Portuguese fried fish is a whole fish or "aku bone" dusted with flour and fried, then doused with vinegary vinha d'ahlos marinade. This version, however, employs lemon juice and a slightly more sophisticated breading, layered with garlic and herbs. Lemon was much used in the days when almost every yard boasted a gnarled old citrus tree, many some unidentifiable lemon or lime cross, but much prized.

As these disappeared, and store-bought lemons rose in price, lemon became less used in Portuguese households. Here, we pair boneless fillets with onion sauce (see page 38). A pound of boneless fish will generously serve 2 to 3; 2 pounds for 4 to 6 people.

1 to 2 pounds moist, white-fleshed, boneless fish fillets (e.g. snapper, monchong, opah, fresh-caught shore fish), $^3/_4$ to 1-inch thick
2 cloves garlic, minced (more if you like)
$^1/_2$ teaspoon salt (divided use)
$^1/_4$ teaspoon pepper (divided use)
Juice and zest of one lemon
3 eggs, separated
$^1/_2$ cup flour (divided use)
2 tablespoons fine cornmeal
Vegetable oil for frying
1 recipe onion sauce (page 38)
Piri-piri (page 36)

Place the fish in a flat baking dish. Rub with garlic, sprinkle with $^1/_4$ teaspoon salt and $^1/_8$ teaspoon pepper. Sprinkle with lemon juice and lemon zest. Marinate 15 minutes; turn and marinate another 15 minutes.

In a small bowl, with a hand-held mixer or whisk, beat 3 egg whites to soft peaks. Set aside.

In a medium bowl or a flat baking dish, beat 3 egg yolks. Place ¼ cup flour and 2 tablespoons cornmeal in a hand-held strainer; slowly and gradually shake flour and cornmeal into yolks, whisking to prevent lumps.

Heat 2 inches of vegetable oil to 365°F in a wok or other heavy-bottomed open pan. (Lacking a thermometer, test oil by throwing a pinch flour on top; oil is hot enough flour floats and sizzles, but doesn't burn.)

Heat oven to warm (150°F). Line a heat-proof baking dish with paper towels.

Working gently, fold whites into yolk mixture to make egg batter.

Lift each fillet from marinade (reserve marinade) and drag through egg batter; dust each with a bit of the remaining flour and place into 365°F oil. Use a Chinese wire ladle or heat-proof slotted spoon to turn and remove fish when it's golden (do not allow to brown). Fry fish one or two pieces at a time; do not crowd.

Remove to paper towel-lined dish and keep warm in oven while you fry fish. If desired, drizzle reserved lemon marinade over fish. Serve with warm onion sauce (spread beneath or spoon on top, as desired). If you like spice, finish with a drizzle of piri-piri (page 36) over the top.

BAKED WHOLE FISH
Makes 6 servings

O ne of the simplest recipes in the Portuguese repertoire is marinated whole, baked fish. A less expensive fish is fine for this dish; it's a shame to mask the flavor of a costly seafood with the intense vinha d'ahlos marinade.

Olive oil
1 whole (3 to 4 pound) fish, gutted, cleaned, head on or off
   as desired
1 recipe vinha d'ahlos marinade (page 41)

With a very sharp knife, make a diagonal slice on either side of the fish and a lengthwise slit in the bottom of the cavity from which the innards were removed. Place fish in plastic storage container with a lid. Pour marinade into and over fish. Marinate overnight, covered, in the refrigerator. Pour a little olive oil into in a roasting pan or an enameled cast iron Dutch oven.

Drain, reserving marinade, and arrange fish in oiled pan or Dutch oven. Bake at 350°F 45 minutes to 1 hour, spooning marinade over from time to time. Bring remaining marinade to a boil, then remove from heat. Serve fish hot with marinade on the side.

Rolos de Atom
TUNA-STUFFED ROLLS

For sandwiches, Portuguese favor a crusty roll similar to the one for which Cuba is famed: hard on the outside, soft and white on the inside, football-shaped. Grandma never made these; we used thick slices of white Portuguese bread. Make the bread yourself (page 167) or buy something similiar in a bakery for this gorgeous tuna sandwich. I've given no ingredient amounts because you can make this for one or a dozen, depending on how much bread and tuna you have.

Crusty, soft-centered rolls
Anchovy paste
Green mayonnaise*
Arugula leaves or mesclun-type baby leaf salad
Ripe, sliced beefsteak tomatoes
Fresh tuna slices (as from a sashimi block), rubbed with
  garlic and seared
Thick-sliced bacon, fried crisp and finely chopped

Break open rolls, leaving one side hinged. Slather with anchovy paste on one side and green mayonnaise on the other. Mound some greens on one side, a tomato slice on the other. Fill each roll with a slice or two of broiled or fried tuna and scatter chopped bacon over. One or two rolls per serving.

* To make green mayonnaise, purée fresh leaves of watercress together with commercial or homemade mayonnaise (the latter is better).

Mollusca Portugueza
CLAMS, MUSSELS OR ABALONE, PORTUGUESE-STYLE
Makes 4 servings

This dish can be made with clams or mussels. Or, use farmed Kona abalone, so popular at farmers markets. In that case, very briefly steam the shucked abalone, or grill it and top with the prepared sauce. I don't recommend canned Top Shell as a substitute.

1 tablespoon olive oil
1 tablespoon butter
1 bay leaf, crumbled
4 cloves garlic, crushed
½ onion, peeled and thinly sliced
½ length or ring of Portuguese sausage, case peeled off, finely chopped
4 pounds fresh clams or mussels
2 peeled, seeded and diced tomatoes
1 cup white wine
2 tablespoons parsley, minced
Splash of vinegar (white or cider)
Dash sea salt
Dash pepper

Scrub and wash clams or mussels; strip beards from mussels, if using. Do not use mussels or that are open and won't close when tapped.

In a large sauté pan, heat olive oil and butter over medium heat. Add bay leaf, garlic, onions and sausage and sauté until onion is wilted and sausage lightly browned. Add clams or mussels and tomatoes; cover and cook gently a few minutes, until all are opened. Add wine, parsley and splash of vinegar. Taste, add salt and pepper. Using tongs, pick out bay leaf. Serve immediately.

SALMON GRAVY

Makes 4 servings

This tomato-salmon stew was once ubiquitous. Even my family, which didn't much like fish, served it often. It was just canned salmon in onions and tomatoes, sometimes with potatoes added to bulk it up. Or it might be served over rice. For elders, it brings back another time.

   1 tablespoon olive oil
   2 onions, sliced and broken into crescents
   2 bunches parsley, chopped
   1 tablespoon garlic, chopped
   2 green onions, sliced thin
   1 (14.5-ounce) can chopped tomatoes (or equivalent ripe, peeled, seeded tomatoes or frozen solid-pack tomatoes)
   2 cans (7.5-ounces each) canned salmon, drained and picked over for bones
   2 potatoes, peeled, diced, and lightly steamed
   Piri piri (page 36) or hot sauce

In a large, open sauté pan, heat the olive oil over medium heat and sauté onions, parsley, garlic and green onion until wilted. Add salmon, tomatoes and potatoes, turn down heat and simmer gently until heated through. Lightly toss the mixture from time to time, to break up the salmon and distribute the ingredients so as not to reduce the salmon to tiny shreds. Serve hot on rice with piri piri or hot sauce as desired.

Grao, Milho, Arroz, Feijão

GRAINS, CORNMEAL, RICE, BEANS

For the average Portugese, grains of all kinds are a significant source of nutrition and protein, particularly cornmeal and beans. Ask any Portuguese about old-time memories and these will come to mind.

MEMORIES FROM
A PORTUGUESE HOUSEHOLD

Years ago, when the Hawaiian Electric Company employed a team of home economists to teach people to use their electric appliances, they also offered free public cooking classes, which continued into the 1990s. They employed non-professionals as well as chefs and home economists, among them a skilled home cook, Eleanora Cambra Cadinha of Kāne'ohe.

One day a decade or so ago, Eleanora and her cousin, Haroldine Nunes Garcia, sat down with me at Eleanora's home to talk-story about Portuguese Hawai'i cooking. The two grew up together; their mothers were sisters. Eleanora lived in Kapahulu and went to St. Patrick's Catholic school; Garcia, a little farther toward town, went to Roosevelt. They watched their elders cook, and helped whenever called upon.

"I love to cook," said Eleanora, "I just like to try different things."

My enduring memory of that day is Eleanora demonstrating her family's Portuguese bread technique. "They started with 10 pounds of flour," she recalled, using a three-rise technique. But it was the kneading part that floored me—and her. Painfully, she knelt and bent over an imaginary alguidar (a large, rectangular, porcelain-lined metal basin, white with a black rim; everyone had them then). She began to lift an imaginary batch of dough over her head and SLAM it into the basin.

She didn't sedately push, fold and turn. She lifted, slammed, pounded with closed fists; pushed, lifted, slammed, pounded. Eleanora would draft her husband, or one of the children, to hold the vessel so it wouldn't huli across the floor. "I don't do it now because I'm too old," she said, laughing.

Garcia once asked her mother what made the old-time Portuguese white bread so good. "Sweat," her mother said, briskly.

They recalled the everyday foods of their childhood. Haroldine said that when they had fried pork chops with bread, her papa would heat the drippings to fry his bread. "I think that was one of my father's crazy food ideas," she said (fried bread is, in fact, traditional with some Portuguese meat dishes).

Both women said their fathers were crazy for parsley, cilantro, and mint. Cooked potatoes were always dressed with mint and parsley, or cilantro and parsley, Hawaiian chili peppers, butter and olive oil.

Eleanora remembered demonstrating her family's Midnight Soup during a holiday show for the Portuguese Pioneer Civic Association, made the day before Christmas at a time when the Catholic church required several hours of fasting before one could receive Holy Communion.

"All day we would be smelling the soup," recalled Eleanora. "And then, after Mass, we would be sitting down to this soup of vermicelli, chicken, vegetables and tomatoes. Oh! It was so good."

For feast days, Eleanora said, there was pão doce (sweetbread), malassadas for Shrove Tuesday (the day before Lent begins), or her mother's treasured fruitcake. "She would make very good biscuits, crispy on the outside and soft on the inside."

Haroldine recalled, as many elder Portuguese would in my interviews, how housewives would tie up their hair in white cloths or kitchen towels before intensive cooking chores or at pig slaughtering time. As a small girl, she said, she'd all but run screaming: "I didn't like that. It reminded me of something spooky!"

They spoke of boiled dinners with ingredients varying from sausage to beef to chicken to all three, with potatoes, cabbage and other vegetables. Haroldine's mother added a little salt pork. Corned beef became the centerpiece after the Portuguese began westernizing their cooking.

Ingredients would be steamed and then baked; the rich, fatty sauce skimmed from the top to serve with the meats and vegetables, the remaining liquid turned into soup next day with the addition of vegetables and watercress.

"Cozido (boiled dinner)," said Eleanora in a soft voice, "that was the meal I cooked for my mother the night before she died."

Portuguese are fond of stuffing (as they are of anything made with bread, truth be told). Eleanora makes hers from scratch and it's the work of days, involving from-scratch broth, ground meats, chopped vegetables, olives, nuts, spices, dried cranberries, crouton-size cubes of dried bread and eggs to bind the whole. This is baked on its own, never in the turkey. "If you stuff it, it pulls all the water out of the meat," Eleanora said.

"Some people put Portuguese sausage," she added. "My mother didn't, so I don't."

To save oven space, she keeps her stuffing warm in an electric wok while she roasts a huge turkey. When I complimented her on this clever solution, she quipped, "Hey! Us Portuguese cooks are smart!"

LEMON POTATOES

Makes 6 servings

Portuguese make generous use of rice, but it's long-grain white rice, not the short- or medium-grain Japanese-style rice. It's used in everything from soups to desserts (rice pudding) and is more likely to be baked than steamed. When the forno (masonry oven) was in use, they put rice in a panela no forno (a ceramic casserole) with boiling water or broth as the oven was cooling down after the bread was removed. It would be done in 20 minutes.

Although rice, cornmeal porridge and bread are the most common starches, potatoes do sometimes play the side-dish roll, as in this easy, sprightly recipe. Use red, tan or golden "salad" potatoes, not baking potatoes.

3 pounds new potatoes, peeled, boiled or steamed and quartered
¼ cup butter
Pinch EACH of flour and nutmeg
Grated rind and juice of 1 lemon
Salt and pepper to taste
1 teaspoon chives, minced
Juice of 1 lemon

Peel and boil potatoes. Drain and reserve; keeping warm. Melt butter; whisk in flour and nutmeg. Add lemon zest and sprinkle with salt and pepper. Cook 1 minute. Add potatoes and roll them around in the sauce. Add chives and drizzle with juice of lemon. Serve warm.

Manuel and Doris Correia will bake in a forno like the outdoor oven they have in their Kalihi backyard, above, during the Smithsonian-sponsored American Folk Life festival in Washington, D.C. (June 14, 1989.)

FRIED RICE-POTATO CAKES
Makes 6 to 8 servings (one or two cakes per person)

These fried rice-potato squares are served with meats or fish at dinner or—my favorite—at breakfast with an over-easy egg, drizzled with piri piri chili sauce. Note that it's a two-day process; the rice mixture sets in the refrigerator and is fried next day. In testing this dish, I've had the occasional failure, where the cakes just wouldn't hold together; so I just put big dollops into my frying pan, browned one side, turned the cake and didn't worry about the shape; it was still delicious.

> 3 cups water or chicken stock
> 1½ cups long-grain rice
> 2 medium salad potatoes, peeled and cut into ⅛-inch squares
> 1 tablespoon bacon drippings, lard or solid shortening, melted
> 1 teaspoon salt
> ½ teaspoon pepper
> 2 tablespoons onion, very finely minced or grated
> 2 tablespoons flat-leaf parsley, very finely minced
> 2 tablespoons flour or fine cornmeal*
> Olive or vegetable oil

Boil water or stock. In a large, heat-proof bowl, combine boiling liquid, rice, potatoes, fat, salt, pepper, onion and parsley. Stir in flour or fine cornmeal. Spread and press the mixture evenly in a large, flat shallow casserole, such as an 11 x 13-inch baking dish. Allow to cool as the rice absorbs the liquid. Refrigerate until set, overnight. With a sharp knife, carefully cut the mixture into squares.

Preheat oven to warm. In a large, heavy-bottomed saute pan (preferably nonstick or well-seasoned cast iron), fry squares, allowing them to brown well. Carefully turn with spatula. Remove to a warm oven as you continue frying cakes. Serve hot.

* Try Arrowhead Mills Organic Yellow Cornmeal, which is quite fine; or process regular cornmeal in a food processor until fine.

Grao, Milho, Arroz, Feijao

RICE SALAD PORTUGUEZA
Makes 8 to 10 servings

R ice salad is often served with roasted or grilled meats or seafood. Start 24 hours in advance, because the recipe works best with day-old rice: steam the rice, cover and chill.

3 cups long-grain rice, cooked and chilled
3 large tomatoes
$1/2$ bunch flat-leaf parsley, minced
4 tablespoons fresh basil, minced
4 cloves garlic, minced
1 red bell pepper, roasted, peeled, chopped
1 cup tender asparagus tips, briefly steamed, finely chopped
$1/4$ cup ripe (black) olives, seeded and sliced

For the vinaigrette:
Tomato water and tomato juice to make up $1/2$ cup
3 tablespoons red wine vinegar
$1/4$ cup fruity olive oil
Salt and pepper to taste

Place rice in a large mixing bowl and gently break up any clumps. Immerse tomatoes in a large pot of boiling water until skin begins to split. Drain. Peel and halve tomatoes. Working over a fine sieve perched on a bowl, squeeze tomatoes to release seeds and allow the tomato water to drip into the bowl. Reserve these juices; discard seeds and skins. Chop tomatoes roughly. Add to the rice the tomatoes, parsley, basil, garlic, bell pepper, asparagus tips and olives. Set aside.

Make a vinaigrette by combining the tomato water/juice, vinegar and olive oil; whisk or shake. Flavor with salt and pepper to taste (start conservatively; more can be added). Allow to season, turning occasionally, for one hour. Spoon up a bit of the salad mixture; dress it with a little dressing and taste; correct seasonings with more parsley or basil, more garlic, vinegar or salt or pepper, as needed. Dress salad and serve.

PORTUGUESE "SPANISH" RICE
Makes 6 servings

Rice cooked with tomatoes in sauce was an everyday favorite in our household. Grandma froze "solid-pack" tomatoes from Grandpa's garden; I use whatever's on hand—over-the-hill heirloom tomatoes, canned chopped or stewed tomatoes. Grandma made this with salt pork; center-cut bacon (not maple bacon) is a good substitute.

   1 tablespoon salt pork, finely chopped
   1 medium onion, peeled and finely chopped
   1 red or yellow bell pepper, cleaned and finely chopped
   2 cups raw long-grain rice
   4 cups tomato liquid (see note below)
   1 cup chopped tomato, drained (see note below)
   1 teaspoon finely ground black pepper

In a heavy-bottomed frying pan over medium heat, saute salt pork; once some of the fat has melted, saute onion and bell pepper until softened. In a casserole dish, stir together all ingredients, cover and bake at 350°F until liquid is absorbed and rice is cooked through.

Notes: Tomato liquid may consist of the liquid from canned tomatoes; a mixture of half tomato sauce and water or broth; or a 6-ounce can of tomato paste with water or broth or any combination that makes 4 cups. For the chopped tomato, use fresh, canned or frozen in 1/4-inch dice.

BAKED RICE, PORTUGUESE-STYLE

This is very a common method of preparing rice throughout the southern Mediterranean. I learned it from an article by the late New York Times *writer* Pierre Franey. The better quality and more flavorful the broth, the better this dish. It's great for entertaining; you can put it in the oven and forget it while you're serving appetizers or socializing.

¼ **cup butter (or olive oil, if you want to be a bit healthier)**
1 **small onion, chopped**
½ **bunch flat-leaf parsley, chopped (optional)**
2 **cups long-grain white rice**
4 **cups boiling chicken broth**

Preheat oven to 325°F. In a Dutch oven or other heatproof vessel, melt butter and gently caramelize onions (and parsley, if using) over medium-low heat. Turn heat up to medium, stir in rice and cook, stirring, until rice is a bit tweedy-looking. Add boiling chicken broth. Cover and place in preheated oven and cook 20 to 25 minutes, until liquid is absorbed.

Variations:

- Fifteen minutes into the cooking, add 1 can drained chopped tomatoes.

- Make a seafood version by using fish broth instead of chicken broth. For example, if you're serving shrimp, buy fresh unpeeled shrimp; toss the peeled shells and heads into a pot of water and make a fish stock. If you can get fish bones, make the broth with those.

Arroz Verde
GREEN RICE
Makes 8 to 10 servings

This green rice is frequently served as a bed for white meats and roasted or grilled fish. Note that you begin with cooked rice.

6 cups steamed long-grain rice
1 pound fresh spinach (stems trimmed) or 1 bag baby spinach
¼ cup green onion , minced
1 teaspoon salt
1 teaspoon curry powder
1 cup half-and-half (may use nonfat half-and-half)
2 eggs, beaten

Preheat oven to 350°F. In a bowl, mix all ingredients well. Butter a casserole dish large enough to accommodate all ingredients. Bake at 350°F 30 to 40 minutes.

DRUNKEN RICE
Serves 6

Here's a baked "pilaf" that's a bit sexier than plain baked rice.

½ cup butter, softened
1 medium onion, chopped
3 tablespoons flat-leaf parsley, minced, plus a little more for
    garnish
2 tablespoons green onion tops, minced
2 cups long-grain white rice, uncooked
3 cups boiling chicken broth
1 cup amontillado sherry (or dry white wine such as vinho
    verde or pinot grigio; do not use cooking sherry, as this
    has added salt)
Parsley for garnish

In a large sauté pan, melt butter and stir in onion, parsley and green onion. Add rice and stir over medium-high heat until rice begins to turn color. Rice will be golden with a few flecks of light brown. Spread rice evenly in a large, heavy casserole dish or a 9 x 13-inch pan. Pour broth and sherry over the rice. Bake at 350°F for 30 minutes or until liquid is absorbed and rice is tender. Garnish with minced parsley or whole parsley leaves.

Milho
CORNMEAL PORRIDGE
Makes 4 to 6 servings

One of the beloved foods of old-time Portugal that's been all but lost is milho, cornmeal, made into a polenta-like porridge, fried into savory cakes, formed into sweet or savory croquettes, baked in a yeast bread, used to thicken soups. White was preferred, but yellow is fine. The trick to smooth, properly cooked milho is to soak some of the cornmeal in water before bringing the mixture to a boil and then to add the remainder in a light, steady stream while stirring. Watch out! Boiling cornmeal tends to spit; turn the heat down as soon as it boils.

4 cups water
1 cup cornmeal, white or yellow
2 tablespoons butter
1/2 teaspoon salt
1 cup Portuguese cabbage or collard greens, julienned

In a roomy saucepan, whisk together water and 1/2 cup of the cornmeal. Place pot over medium heat and add butter and salt. Bring to a boil, stirring constantly. Reduce heat to medium; pour remaining cornmeal in in a steady stream, whisking constantly. Cook over medium heat 10 minutes, stirring; add greens and cook a further 5 to 10 minutes. Serve as a side dish with fish or meats.

Variation: Instead of greens, use 1/2 cup minced flat-leaf parsley.

Milho Frito
FRIED CORNMEAL PORRIDGE

For many Portuguese, a milho side dish was just an excuse to make fried cornmeal slices, served the next day at breakfast with eggs, fried chunks of leftover vinha d'ahlos (pickled pork) and salty olives. Cooks routinely made double batches; some to be eaten as porridge, some to be fried.

Milho (see recipe on page 133), still warm and soft
Butter
Vegetable or olive oil, for frying

Butter a baking dish or loaf pan and evenly spread the hot cooked meal in it. Refrigerate at least half a day or overnight. Slice or cut into squares and fry over medium-high heat in vegetable or olive oil until golden and crisp (a nonstick pan helps). Serve at breakfast with fried eggs (and leftover vinha d'ahlos, if you have any).

SPICY TOMATO FAVAS, LIMAS OR EDAMAME

Makes 6 servings

Fava beans (aka broad or horse beans) are a favorite in the southern Mediterranean, but are hard to find in Hawai'i and expensive. Limas, or even edamame (soybeans) can stand in. If you do find fresh favas, soak them overnight in cold water, then boil until tender; you can also find them canned online. Gorgeous fresh, vari-colored lima beans (cream and burgundy, not green) can sometimes be found at Filipino stands in Chinatown or in farmers markets.

- 1 cup chopped ham, linguiça (Portuguese sausage) or pancetta
- 1 small onion, finely chopped
- 3 cloves garlic, minced
- 1/8 teaspoon cayenne pepper
- 1/2 teaspoon paprika
- 2 small, hot Hawaiian chili peppers (ni'oi), minced
- 1 (6-ounce) can tomato paste
- 3 cups hot water or chicken broth
- 1 pound (2 cups) canned fava beans, fresh or frozen lima or frozen pre-cooked edamame (soy beans)
- 1/4 cup red wine vinegar
- Salt and pepper to taste

In a large saute pan, lightly brown chopped ham, linguiça or pancetta. Add onion, garlic, spices and peppers and saute. Stir in tomato paste and water or broth. Bring to a gentle simmer and add beans. Cook until beans are tender about 15 to 25 minutes, depending on whether the beans were fresh or frozen, raw or precooked. Splash in red wine vinegar; add salt and pepper. Taste and correct seasonings.

HOT GARBANZO SALAD
Makes 6 to 8 servings

G arbanzos, aka chickpeas, are used in soups, braised meat dishes and in salads like this, a melange of beans and our beloved bacalhao, salt cod. Rich in protein, this salad might actually serve as an entrée for an informal meal.

1 tablespoon olive oil
1 small onion, minced
1 cup green onion, ¼-inch slice (green and white parts)
¼ teaspoon ground black pepper
½ teaspoon paprika
2 (5-ounce) bottles clam juice or equivalent homemade fish stock
Juice of 1 lemon
2 (15.25-ounce) cans cooked garbanzo beans
1 (15.25-ounce) can kidney beans
1 cup soaked, picked over, briefly simmered and flaked salt cod (See Aperetivos, page 114)
2 hard-boiled eggs
Salt and pepper (just a couple of pinches of each)

Heat olive oil over medium heat in a large, heavy-bottomed skillet. Add onion and green onion, pepper and paprika; cook until onions and green onion are wilted. Add clam juice or stock and lemon juice; cook 5 minutes. Add beans and salt cod and cook until heated through. Meanwhile, separate yolks from whites. Slice or grate whites and crumble egg yolks. Place salad in a wide, shallow serving bowl and top with egg slices and crumbles. Sprinkle with salt and pepper. Serve hot.

PORTUGUESE BAKED BEANS
Makes 6 servings

These baked beans are quite different from the sweet, brown sugary baked beans most of us are used to.

2 cups dry navy beans
Water
1 (10-ounce) length linguiça
1 onion, chopped
2 cloves garlic
½ cup parsley, chopped
1 cup strong coffee
1 (1-inch) piece salt pork
1 (6-ounce) can tomato paste
½ cup raw sugar
1 cup port wine
1 tablespoon grainy mustard

In a large soup pot, soak navy beans overnight in water to cover by at least 2 inches. Drain and place in soup pot with fresh water to cover. Bring beans to a boil, skim foam and cook, simmering 60 to 90 minutes, until beans are tender. Preheat oven to 300°F. Meanwhile, slice and brown linguiça lightly; remove sausage, set aside, and saute onions, garlic and parsley over medium to medium-low heat, just until wilted and soft. Drain beans, reserving liquid for later use. In a large, heat-proof casserole dish, place beans, linguiça, onion, garlic, parsley, coffee, salt pork, tomato paste, sugar, wine and mustard in the casserole and stir well to distribute ingredients. If the mixture is dry, add ½ to 1 cup bean liquid; the mixture should be slushy but not soupy. Bake at 300°F for 60 to 90 minutes. (About 45 minutes into cooking time, check liquid level, taste liquid and correct seasonings.)

Shortcut version: Combine 2 large cans pork and beans, 1 recipe refogado (page 71), coffee, raw sugar, port and mustard and bake as above.

Bread-based dishes variously known as migas (when soupy) and recheio (when more like Thanksgiving stuffing) were not just a holiday food. They were a way to use up dry bread, which was always on hand because the simple, almost fat-free breads baked in the forno had a short shelf life, becoming as hard as rocks within days. Also used: other leftovers—bits of meat, ends of onions and vegetables, broth or soup. To use fresh bread, cut it into slices; place it on a baking sheet and dry it in a 325°F oven until crisp.

The Portuguese forno, a community oven, appeared on many sugar plantations throughout the islands. This photo was taken around 1890.

Recheio might be a side dish at dinner, a base for poached eggs at breakfast, combined with mashed potatoes or cooked vegetables, or moistened with leftover gravy and baked.

Tip: Recheio, the Portuguese word for stuffing, is pronounced "roo-SHAYD-oo." Who knew?

Recheio I
SIMPLE LEFTOVER STUFFING
Makes 6 to 8 servings

1 tablespoon olive or vegetable oil or bacon drippings
1 pound cooked meats, bacon, sausage or ham, chopped
1 cup onions, chopped
1 cup celery, chopped
½ cup flat-leaf parsley, minced
2 garlic cloves, minced
10 to 12 cups chunks of dried bread
4 cups liquid (broth, stock, leftover plain soup, white
   wine—in whatever proportion desired)
½ teaspoon salt
¼ teaspoon pepper

In a heavy-bottomed Dutch oven, heat oil or bacon fat and brown meats. Transfer meat to paper towels to drain; remove all but a tablespoon of fat from the pot if any has been rendered. Place onions, celery, parsley and garlic in hot fat and cook to wilt, 5 to 10 minutes. Preheat oven to 325°F.

In a very large bowl, combine meat and vegetables with dried bread chunks. Stirring and tossing, drizzle in liquid until bread is moistened but not wet or soupy (you may not need all the liquid). Place the recheio in a large buttered casserole and bake at 325°F until heated through.

Variations: Add a can of chopped or stewed tomatoes when you combine the vegetables and bread. Add 1 or 2 minced small, hot red chili peppers when you saute the vegetables.

O Recheio de Minha Comadre
MY GODMOTHER'S STUFFING
Makes 8 to 10 cups

very Christmas, on my holiday visit to Maui, my godmother, Cyril-la Medeiros, would save me a dish of her unconventional stuffing, made with pickled roast beef. I tend to take the bowl, hug it to my chest and begin snarling like a canine protecting a bone. To make this recipe, you need a meat grinder, or must to chop everything very, very fine; the surfaces of the various ingredients have to get up close and personal to achieve the right flavor and texture.

1 turkey neck
Water
Vinha D'ahlos Roast Beef (recipe follows)
2 rings or lengths (10 to 12 ounces each) spicy-hot Portu-
guese sausage
1 onion
5 to 6 cloves garlic
½ bunch flat-leaf parlsey
10 cups plain, dry bread for stuffing (not crumbs, small
squares)
1 cup pitted green olives, chopped

Place the turkey neck in twice as much water as needed to cover; bring to a boil and reduce until the turkey neck is almost uncovered. Reserve this stock; discard neck. Cut roast into thirds. Grind or very finely chop one-third, or until you have 2 to 3 cups. (There will be leftovers for other uses.) Grind or very finely mince the Portuguese sausage. Do the same with the onion, garlic and parsley.

In a very large bowl combine beef, sausage, onion, garlic and parsley with bread chunks and olives. Drizzle with turkey water to moisten while you toss stuffing. It should be damp but not wet. Spread the stuffing in a buttered baking dish and bake at 350°F until heated through and browned. Or stuff turkey and bake whatever doesn't fit in bird.

VINHA D'AHLOS ROAST BEEF
Makes 10 to 12 servings

Auntie Cyrilla would make a gigando roast and uses the leftovers in a variety of ways to cut down on cooking after the holiday madness.

Auntie Cyrilla Medeiros

8 pounds sirloin tip roast, stripped of fat
4 cups cider vinegar
4 cups water
2 to 3 fresh red hot Hawaiian chili peppers, (niʻoi), finely minced
2 to 3 cloves garlic
½ teaspoon salt

In a large, non-reactive bowl or plastic container, marinate roast in vinegar and water with chilies, garlic and salt overnight, covered. Drain. Roast at 350°F until cooked through (155°F internal temperature).

Salades e Legumes
SALADS, VEGETABLES

Portuguese salads are not the sort that we think of in America; few greens, many vegetables. We don't necessarily serve them as a first course; they are often served as a second or third course between the appetizer and the fish or meat.

THE LOST BEAN

One day, the phone rang at *The Honolulu Advertiser* and it was a man named Roy Camara. He told me he was older and had just one thing left on his foodie "bucket list": to taste again what sounded to me like "tagamooszh."

Once my mind had run the word through my pitifully inadequate Portuguese filter, I realized he meant tremoço—lupin (aka lupine) beans (lupini to the Italians).

"They sold them at the Holy Ghost fair," he said. "You used to be able to buy the dry beans in the Japanese stores."

The beans were beloved of Portuguese men, who ate tremoço salgado (salted lupin beans) as a snack with small glasses of homemade wine or, later, beer. I suspect they weren't so beloved of Portuguese women because lupin beans are very high in alkaloids and naturally terribly bitter, so they must be soaked, washed, boiled and boiled again to make them sweet and soft.

I sighed. The Holy Ghost fairs are largely gone (there's one left, on the Big Island), and the dried beans are available only online. You can find them bottled in brine at some specialty food stores (R. Field). I was to hear many more times while researching this book about the beloved tremoços.

These small, cream-colored or mottled beans have a thin skin that's part of the fun. You pick them up, squeeze one end and pop the bean out onto your tongue. They're the edamame of the Portuguese!

They are also a very ancient, agriculturally important and nutritious food, found in Egyptian tombs, eaten in Roman

Principals in the Holy Ghost Feast (about 1920) celebrated annually by the Portuguese residents of Honomu Plantation on the Big Island. Most of the Portuguese people who arrived in Hawai'i brought with them firm religious convictions and a strong sense of community solidarity.

times, treasured by the Incas, used everywhere as a soil-feeding crop and ground cover as well as a food.

They're high in protein, rich in fiber and carotenes, as well as calcium and "good" oils. They are preserved in brine in Italy, France, Portugal and North Africa. The Italians use dried and ground lupins to make a pasta. They're mixed with semolina to make little cakes in Europe and South America. And when you're done with the cooking water, you can throw it on the garden to deter insects and snails while feeding the plants.

The plants do need some cold hours, so might grow well here only in the higher elevations, but what a plant worthy of a revival! If you find bottled lupini, drain, rinse and dry them, sprinkle with sea salt and grab a glass of red table wine to go with.

This article owes much to "Cultural practices and production constraints in lupines." 1987. S. J. Herbert. In Grain Legumes as Alternative Crops, a symposium sponsored by the Center for Alternative Crops and Products. Univ. of Minn., July 23-24, 1987. 194 pp. and to various non-copyrighted articles recently scanned for online use that tell of Azorean and Madeiran agricultural practices in the 19th century and to date.

Grelos
SAUTEED PORTUGUESE CABBAGE OR COLLARD GREENS
Makes 4 servings

Couves was Grandma's fallback vegetable; we always had an entire row of Portuguese cabbage ready for harvest in the garden, and when she couldn't think of anything else for a vegetable, this would be her choice.

> 1 bunch (10 to 12 large leaves) Portuguese cabbage or collard greens
> Extra-virgin olive oil
> 1 to 3 cloves garlic, minced
> ½ sweet onion, finely chopped
> ½ teaspoon salt (or less, to taste)
> Pinch of pepper
> 1 to 2 tablespoons water or chicken stock
> Vinegar or lemon juice, if desired

Wash the greens, trim thick stems, wipe them gently dry and stack them on a cutting board. Roll into a thick cigar and cut crosswise into julienne strips. Set aside. Heat a large, heavy-bottomed saute pan over medium-high heat. Add a good splash of olive oil and heat. Add the minced garlic and sweet onion, turn the heat down to medium and cook until limp and beginning to change color (if the garlics browns, discard it and start again to avoida burnt flavor).

Add the shredded greens and saute until bright green but cooked through, 2 to 4 minutes, adding water or stock as needed to prevent sticking and allowing the greens to steam slightly. Remove from the heat and toss with a generous seasoning of salt and pepper, tasting as you go. Portuguese like a splash of vinegar or squeeze of lemon juice on top but don't apply the acid until right before serving as the vegetables will turn gray.

(continued on the next page)

Tip: Funchal, the capital city of Madeira, and the place from which many Hawai'i Portuguese ancestors embarked, is named for fennel, the anise-flavored, celery-like vegetable. Try it where you would use celery and see what you think. It cooks quickly, either sautéed or braised.

GREEN BEANS WITH LINGUIÇA
Makes 4 servings

One of my favorite old-timey Honolulu restaurants, Henry Loui's, serves a version of this as a pūpū. Eat it with your fingers or serve it as a vegetable side dish.

1 tablespoon olive oil
6 ounces (about ½ length) linguiça sausage
6 tablespoons light olive oil
¼ cup fresh lemon juice
¼ teaspoon salt
Pinch pepper
1 pound fresh green beans, trimmed
Lemon wedges or slices for garnish

Heat 1 tablespoon olive oil. Cut the casing from the sausage and crumble into hot oil; fry until just slightly crisp. Drain on paper towels and set aside. Make a vinaigrette with the olive oil and lemon juice; add salt to taste. Boil a large pot of water. Plunge the fresh green beans into the boiling water and cook just until they are bright green but still somewhat crunchy. Immediately drain the beans and plunge into a pot of ice water to stop the cooking. Drain well and pat dry.

Place in a serving platter and drizzle with lemon vinaigrette. Top with fried Portuguese sausage crumbles. Garnish with lemon and serve.

Salades e Legumes

GREEN MOUSSE
WITH ROASTED TOMATOES
Makes 4 to 6 servings

I n classic French circles, the term "a la Portugues" means a dish that features tomatoes. Stuffed tomatoes are a classic. Here, they're made with spinach but baby kale would do as well.

1 pound fresh, washed spinach leaves
2 tablespoons extra-virgin olive oil
1 tablespoon flour
1 clove garlic, cut into three slices
Lemon juice or wine vinegar
$1/2$ teaspoon salt
$1/4$ teaspoon pepper
4 to 6 medium to small whole tomatoes
Olive oil
Flat-leaf parsley or cilantro

Quickly steam the spinach leaves; drain in colander, press out water, and chop. In a heavy-bottomed frying pan, heat olive oil over medium heat; add garlic pieces and swirl to flavor oil, continuing just until garlic is golden. Discard garlic pieces. Whisk flour into olive oil and cook 1 minute. Add spinach and cook a couple of minutes. Season with lemon juice or wine vinegar and salt.

Preheat oven to 400°F. Cut the stem-end tops from the tomatoes and spoon out meat. Place shells on a foil-lined cookie sheet drizzled with olive oil and roast until tomatoes are heated through and even a little browned at the edges. Remove from oven, fill the tomato cavities with spinach mixture and return to oven. Remove when heated through and garnish with minced flat-leaf parsley or cilantro. Serve immediately as a dinner side dish.

COUVES • PORTUGUESE CABBAGE: MY MISSION IN LIFE

Taking an evening stroll in my brother's Kaʻaʻawa neighborhood a few years back, I peeked over a fence and cried, "Look! Portuguese cabbage! I haven't seen that since Grandpa's garden."

"Oh, yeah," he said, "that's Gerard Vincent's. I bet he'd let you have some."

I finally got up the courage to ask if Mr. Vincent would start a plant for me, and he said there was nothing simpler: Just stick a cutting in the dirt. Now, I've got Portuguese cabbage plants thriving in pots.

Portuguese cabbage is among many all-but-forgotten forms of ethnic produce that once flourished in backyard gardens here. Portuguese call cabbage "couves" (KOOV-zsh). But by that, they don't mean the tight, rolled heads of standard cabbage.

Portuguese cabbage is broad-leafed and bright green with white midribs, the leaves growing in a spiral around

Tony & me

a central stalk. It is generally called couve tronchuda (a corruption of Trauxuda, the region of Portugal from which it was first imported) but it might also be called couve Galega. According to gardening resources, its family name is *Brassica oleracea* var. *costata*.

Although you can substitute kale for Portuguese cabbage, I prefer collard greens because they come closer to the tender and delicate texture of Portuguese cabbage. This went into our Portuguese bean soup. And it is the main ingredient in the national soup of Portugal, caldo verde ("green soup").

I found an online source for seeds: Redwood City Seeds (650-325-7333, www.ecoseeds.com). Or just try to find a friendly Portuguese gardener who will cut you a slip, like my pal, Mr. Vincent.

I've made it my mission to make cuttings, or steal them from my cousin, Tony Duarte, in Kāneʻohe. His cabbages were the size of bushes, almost taller than me! These I've given to farmers, gardening enthusiasts, anyone who shows interest. I want this ridiculously easy-to-grow plant to flourish again in home gardens.

LEGUMES A SALADES

The classic Portuguese salad is unremarkable, in that it's unchanging, available everywhere and everywhere wonderful. The simple ingredients are fresh and full of flavor, ripe with the coveted balance of sugar to acid. Don't try a salad like this without the best possible ingredients.

All you need: salt-sprinkled cucumber strips, allowed to weep out their liquid then wiped free of visible salt; sliced roasted bell pepper, chunks of tomato, thinly sliced olives and a plain vinaigrette, laid out attractively rather than tossed.

The conventional American salad of raw greens is little seen in Portugal. Most salads more closely resemble entrées or side dishes.

The invariable dressing is a vinaigrette, made with wine or cider vinegar, lemon or other citrus juices, occasionally a creamy housemade mayonnaise or a sweet-sour blend made with the lees of local wine.

EGGPLANT, PUMPKIN AND SWEET POTATO "TEMPURA"

Makes 6 pūpū servings

Like Southerners, Portuguese tend to take healthy vegetables and do their worst with them—that is, add delicious fat and salt. Desculpa! (Sorry!)

It's said that it was Portuguese mariners, or possibly missionaries, who taught the Japanese to batter-fry, creating the distinctly Japanese dish known as tempura. Here's a Portuguese version.

1 egg
1 cup flour
2 teaspoons salt
Ice water, as needed
Flaked sea salt
2 long Japanese eggplant, ends trimmed
1 medium kabocha pumpkin (about 1½ pounds)
3 small orange sweet potatoes or Okinawan sweet potatoes
Pure olive oil for frying

In a medium mixing bowl, whisk together egg, flour and salt to make a thickish batter; add a few drops ice water as needed to make it loose enough for dipping. Cover and refrigerate. Cut eggplant crosswise into 1/4-inch rounds; salt and allow to "weep" in a colander in the sink for 30 minutes. With paper towels, wipe away moisture and salt.

Microwave whole, unpeeled kabocha pumpkin 7 to 10 minutes. Slice pumpkin in half, scrape out seeds and strings and peel skin. Microwave an additional 5 to 6 minutes until pumpkin is fully cooked but not mushy. Cut pumpkin halves in half, then into 1/4-inch slices. Salt very lightly.

In a large pot of boiling, salted water, boil sweet potatoes until fork-tender; cool and peel and cut into 1/3-inch slices (if the potatoes are very thick, cut these slices in half).

Preheat oven to lowest possible temperature. Heat 2 to 3 inches of olive oil to 350°F in a large, heavy-bottomed pot, such as a Dutch oven. Dip eggplant, pumpkin or potatoes pieces one by one into chilled batter and fry in a single, uncrowded layer; remove with Chinese straining ladle; drain on paper towels. Place on heat-proof platter in warm oven and serve alongside grilled or roasted meats or baked and grilled seafood.

OLIVE AND BELL PEPPER SALAD
Makes 4 servings

This is a typical Portuguese salad—no leafy greens.

1 bulb fennel
Olive oil
1 clove garlic, minced
1 tablespoon sweet onion, minced
1 red bell pepper
1 yellow bell pepper
1 jar pimiento strips, drained
1 small basket red or yellow or mixed cherry tomatoes, or 2
    large, ripe heirloom tomatoes
1 cup whole Spanish olives (or garlic-stuffed olives)
Juice and zest of 1 lemon
Dash or two of black pepper

Wash and trim the fennel, breaking stalks apart and slicing into 1-inch lengths. Pat dry. Heat the olive oil over medium-high heat. Saute fennel over medium or medium-low heat until edges just begin to brown. Add garlic and sweet onion and saute 30 seconds. Remove from heat, drain on paper towels. Halve bell peppers, remove stem, seeds and membrane, chop into 1-inch squares.

Drain jar of pimiento strips and place on paper towels. Slice cherry tomatoes in half; cut whole tomatoes into chunks.

In a salad bowl, layer vegetables, olives and lemon zest and very lightly toss. Just before serving, drizzle with lemon juice and season with a few twists of freshly ground black pepper.

Esperregado
SPINACH IN WHITE SAUCE
Makes 4 to 6 servings

Trust the Portuguese to make a white sauce not with butter but olive oil, flavored with garlic, warm spices and vinegar as well as the conventional milk. This thin Portuguese-style bechamel can be used with any vegetable, but esperregado (spinach) is traditional.

- **2 bunches spinach or 1 bag baby spinach leaves (6 ounces)**
- **2 tablespoons olive oil**
- **3 cloves garlic**
- **1 tablespoon flour**
- **¼ teaspoon Portuguese 5-Spice (or nutmeg)**
- **2 cups warm milk**
- **2 tablespoons white vinegar**
- **½ teaspoon salt**
- **¼ teaspoon pepper**

Trim off stems if using mature spinach; wash spinach in cold running water. Place the wet spinach in a saucepan or frying pan over medium-high heat and cook until just wilted. Remove to cutting board and chop roughly. Set aside. In a large saute pan over medium heat, heat olive oil and saute garlic until golden. Whisk in flour and 5-Spice and cook gently for 2 minutes. Whisk and stir warm milk into flour mixture and cook 10 minutes until thickened. Add spinach and stir to coat. Splash in vinegar, season with salt and pepper, taste and correct seasonings.

MARINATED EGGPLANT SALAD
Makes 4 to 6 servings

S lim, cucumber-shaped Japanese eggplant has been adopted by many Portuguese in the islands because it grows well here and is much easier to process than bulky globe eggplant. This is a typical cooked salad that depends on the best possible tomatoes to balance the oily richness and creaminess of the fried eggplant.

3 long Japanese eggplant, ends trimmed
$\frac{1}{2}$ teaspoon salt
$\frac{1}{4}$ teaspoon pepper
Pure olive oil for frying
2 cups flour
3 to 5 ripe beefsteak tomatoes, sliced; or equivalent halved
  cherry or grape tomatoes
$\frac{1}{2}$ cup any vinaigrette dressing

Slice eggplant crosswise about $\frac{1}{2}$ inch thick; sprinkle lightly with salt and allow to "weep" in colander in sink for 30 minutes. With paper towels, wipe away moisture and salt. Heat 2 to 3 inches oil in heavy-bottomed pot over medium-high heat to 325°F. Season 2 cups flour with salt and pepper and place in a large, shallow dish. Flour both sides of each slice; fry until golden; drain on paper towels. Place eggplant slices in wide, shallow casserole in a single layer, top with fresh, ripe tomato slices; drizzle with vinaigrette and continue layering. Allow to season $\frac{1}{2}$ hour and serve at room temperature.

Lower fat version: Skip the flour and oil. In a microwave-safe dish with a cover, microwave eggplant slices 8 to 12 minutes (depending on thickness and power of your microwave oven) until fully cooked. Proceed as above, placing eggplant in casserole with tomatoes and vinaigrette.

WATERCRESS AND WALNUT SALAD
Makes 4 to 6 servings

Watercress is a Portuguese favorite, though the variety most widely grown here is leggier and tougher than the lower-growing, more delicate style enjoyed elsewhere. With conventional Island watercress, use the leaves and carefully trim and cut the stems. Here, the peppery taste marries with the bitter creaminess of walnuts.

This salad makes use of a member of a family of dressings that swept the U.S. in the 1950s. widely known as "French" dressing. But it's known in Portugal, too. And loved. Make it in bulk; the recipe here is a famed one in Hawai'i, given to me by a longtime St. Louis High School cafeteria manager, the late Mrs. Eleanor Tyau.

1 bunch watercress
1 cup toasted walnuts
Mrs. Tyau's Dressing (recipe follows)

Boil a large pot of water. Fill another pot or a clean sink with cold water and ice. Pull tender leaves from watercress and reserve. Cut stems into ⅛-inch slices, discarding the most fibrous and woody. Boil stems 15 to 20 seconds. Add leaves and boil an additional 15 to 20 seconds. Drain and stop cooking in cold water. Drain and pat dry with paper towels.

Meanwhile, toast walnuts and rub off dark skin. Chop into medium bits (not too fine, not too chunky; pleasant chewing size). In a bowl, toss watercress with walnuts. Just before serving, sparingly dress room-temperature salad with Mrs. Tyau's Dressing.

Salades e Legumes

MRS. TYAU'S DRESSING

Makes about 2 cups

One key to this and many other dressings and dishes from the same period is grated onion; you used to be able to buy it bottled, it was so common. Hand-grate onions; do not use a food processor. Mrs. Tyau was Korean but there is a Portuguese connection. She was the longtime cafeteria manager at St. Louis High School and those boys, many Portuguese, LOVED her dressing—they ate it on everything.

1 (14.5-ounce) can tomato soup
1 cup salad oil
½ cup vinegar
¼ cup sugar
1 teaspoon salt
1 teaspoon dry mustard
1 teaspoon paprika
3 tablespoons Worcestershire sauce
2 tablespoons onion, grated
1 clove garlic, crushed and minced

Combine all ingredients except garlic in blender; blend until well-mixed. Add garlic and blend until smooth.

MINT VINAIGRETTE
Makes 2 to 4 servings

Mint vinaigrette pairs well with steamed vegetables as well as salads. Be sure to use fragrant, very fresh mint.

3 tablespoons sliced fresh mint
1 clove garlic, minced
4 tablespoons lemon juice
³/₄ cup olive oil
³/₄ teaspoon ground cumin
1 pound very lightly steamed new peas (or frozen peas), still hot
Salt and pepper to taste

In a food processor (a mini-processor works well), pulse together mint, garlic, lemon juice, olive oil and cumin just until minced. Toss with warm peas. Season with salt and pepper; taste and correct seasonings.

Variations: Serve with steamed peas, sugar snap peas, carrots or green beans. Or with a salad of steamed and room-temperature grilled, seared or steamed vegetables.

Note: Use this dressing, minus the mint, on a Mediterranean Salade Niçoise—strips of canned sardine, pieces of seared tuna, boiled potato and egg slices and seeded olives over greens. Though identified with Nice, in France, such a salad would be at home on a Portuguese table as a French one.

LEMON ZUCCHINI

Makes 4 to 6 servings

I've always loathed zucchini: limp and watery when cooked; bitter when raw; too often poorly fried and greasy. Chef Tracy Des Jardins (you saw her on "Top Chef Masters") changed my mind in a cooking demonstration at Kapi'olani Community College in which she shaved firm, young, skin-on zucchini into eye-pleasing thin ribbons. Here, the cutting technique is hers but the vinaigrette is Portuguese.

In Portugal, it's likely the zucchini would be sliced and fried in olive oil, then layered with minced garlic and fresh herbs and dressed with plain boiled white vinegar, a bit sharp and oily for our tastes. Here, we bathe raw zucchini in lemon.

3 to 5 young, firm zucchini
3 tablespoons finely minced flat-leaf parsley
$1/4$ teaspoon kosher salt
$1/8$ teaspoon white pepper

For the vinaigrette:
1 teaspoon sea salt flakes
2 large cloves garlic, minced
$1/2$ teaspoon white pepper
2 teaspoons sugar
4 teaspoons fresh lemon juice
Zest of 1 lemon
$1/4$ cup olive oil

Red, yellow or orange cherry or grape tomatoes, halved (for garnish) OR slivers of jarred pimiento or roasted sweet pepper, drained, slivered

Run unpeeled zucchini lengthwise through a mandoline. Slice crosswise into sticks. Layer with parsley, salt and pepper; refrigerate, covered. Meanwhile, in a mortar, combine the sea salt and garlic and pound to a paste. Add pepper and sugar and grind a bit more. Splash in lemon juice,

(continued on the next page)

drizzle in oil and whisk with fork. Remove zucchini from refrigerator and drain if any water has been released. Pour vinaigrette over zucchini and toss. Marinate overnight. Toss again. Serve in a decorative salad bowl or platter garnished with tomatoes, pimiento or bell pepper.

Tip: When a recipe calls for deep-frying in olive oil, use pure olive oil, the cheapest and least flavorful; don't waste a good, fruity extra-virgin olive oil.

PORTUGUESE PEAS
Makes 4 servings

*I*f Hawai'i were perfect, we'd be able to get fresh English peas. But, alas!, no place is perfect. So you'll have to use frozen peas for this hearty dish that can serve as an entrée for lunch or a light dinner, with good, crusty fresh bread for soaking. Your kids might even eat it.

> 2 tablespoons butter, rendered bacon fat or olive oil
> 1 finely small onion, chopped
> 1 cup chicken broth
> 3 cups frozen peas, lightly steamed
> 2 tablespoons flat-leaf parsley, minced
> 2 tablespoons cilantro, minced
> Pinch sugar
> Pinch salt
> 5 to 6 ounces (about half a length or ring) Portuguese sausage, sliced
> 4 eggs

In a skillet, heat butter, bacon fat or olive oil until melted; sweat onions over medium-low heat until they are relaxed and translucent. Stir in broth, peas, parsley, cilantro, sugar and salt. Cover peas and onions evenly with slices of Portuguese sausage. Bring to a boil; reduce heat to medium and cook gently 5 minutes. With a wooden spoon, make four slight depressions in the mixture. Break an egg carefully into each one; cover and cook until eggs are poached. Serve immediately, carefully using a large open spoon to separate out a portion of egg and spinach.

O Pão
BREAD

Every bread recipe suggests rising in a warm, breeze-free place. This is especially important for lean breads, like broa (yeasted cornbread), and for richer, high-fat doughs like sweetbread. But where is a warm place?

On a hot, humid day, your counter may be a sufficient, so long as you cover the dough. Otherwise, turn the oven on to 150°F just long enough to achieve that temperature. As soon as you hear the heating element click off and the preheat light turns off, switch off the oven. Place the dough in the oven.

A pottery or earthenware bowl is best to hold your rising dough; either material holds heat well (as opposed to metal or glass). Use a bowl that allows room for rising. Cover with a light cloth or buttered or oil-sprayed plastic wrap.

BRICK OVEN

In her childhood, my grandmother baked bread several times a week in a forno, a Portuguese masonry oven, but I'd never done so until a few years ago when the folks at Hawai'i's Plantation Village invited chef Alan Wong and his then-pastry chef, Mark Okumura, to try out their oven with the aid of forno expert Clyde Vierra.

It was a chicken-skin day. But unlike my grandmother, who had to make yeast from potatoes, pound the dough into submission by hand and pray it wouldn't fall or go sour, I could prepare my bread dough in a KitchenAid stand mixer, let it rise overnight in the refrigerator in zip-closure bags, and count on somebody else to handle the fire-building chores.

Vierra learned from Big Island master Abe Baptiste, who helped build this forno (behind the Portuguese house at the Plantation Village). The beehive-shaped oven, made of stone, brick and heat-conducting masonry "mud," hadn't been used in years. Vierra, fearful that we wouldn't be able to get the fire hot enough in rain-soaked oven, had built a fire three days in a row to dry the oven out. It still took a good two hours to bring the thing to the proper temperature.

The forno was a center of Portuguese family life. Father built the ovens. Youngsters gathered the wood. Young girls helped their mothers knead the bread.

Neighbors often shared a single oven. Many women made sold bread, or bartered bread for goods. Once the bread was removed, the residual heat would be used to slow-cook soups or stews or, on special occasions, to roast meats.

Vierra confirmed much that I had heard: That the temperature test for a forno involves throwing a handful of flour onto the floor of the oven. If it blackens immediately, the oven is too hot. If it browns nicely, it's time to bake. If it remains white, uh-oh, you have to build another fire. Wet banana leaves or a cloth mop were used to clean out the oven and help create a steamy environment to encourage a crackling crust.

"What we're talking about here is yesterday's bread," Vierra declared, with a more chewy texture and denser crumb.

Finally, wisps of smoke made their way through cracks in the masonry and the oven's outside walls were warm to the touch. Then it was

Clyde Vierra pulls fresh bread from the Portugese brick oven at Hawai'i's Plantation Village while then Alan Wong's Pastry Chef Mark Okumura grabs them for testing.

time for a frenzy of activity: Vierra used a hoe to rake the coals into a brick bin at the front of the oven, which, by the way, works nicely as a barbecue burner if you pop a grill on top. Once the coals were out, Vierra deployed a mop of wet towels tied to a broom handle to wash away the soot—hot, sweaty, potentially dangerous work.

Okumura had made a half-dozen loaves of Portuguese-style yeasted cornbread, and I'd done two loaves each of various Portuguese white breads. We raced the breads into the oven, using a large stone to prop the oven's heavy cast-iron door shut.

Just less than a half-hour into the baking time, we made the first check. The breads looked gorgeous, puffy and golden-brown. I felt a thrill and sent up a little prayer for whatever wisdom Grandma has bequeathed to me. But the breads were far from done when we checked the internal temperature with an instant-read thermometer: My two largest loaves would take more than 45 minutes, and even Okumura's pie-sized corn loaves needed more cooking time. Vierra gamely opened and shut the oven three times until we could finally taste the fruits of our labors. What a day of channeling the ancestors!

Broa
YEASTED PORTUGUESE CORNBREAD
Makes 1 (9-inch) round loaf

B roa is the forgotten bread of the Portuguese. This simple yeasted cornbread was once baked almost daily, in small loaves suitable for a single meal for the family. Broa is inexpensive, requiring little but cornmeal, flour, olive oil and yeast, and is particularly prized with hearty soups. Important to its success is fine cornmeal; I like Arrowhead Mills Organic Yellow Cornmeal and Bob's Red Mill. This bread does not rise high.

- 1½ tablespoons active dry yeast
- 1 teaspoon sugar
- ¼ cup very warm water
- 1½ cups fine-ground white or yellow cornmeal
- 1 cup very hot water
- 4 teaspoons olive oil
- 2 cups all-purpose flour, plus ½ cup or more for kneading*
- 1½ teaspoons salt

In a small bowl or measuring cup, blend together yeast and sugar and whisk in warm water. Allow to foam and bubble. In a medium bowl, combine cornmeal, hot water and olive oil and blend well. Meanwhile, in a very large bowl, combine flour and salt and whisk together. Stir cornmeal mixture into flour-salt mixture and blend well. Pour in yeast mixture; stir and knead by hand to form ball of dough. Knead until smooth (you can do this right in the bowl). Dough will be slightly wet. Place dough in warm place to rise 60 minutes. Scatter ½ cup flour onto counter; punch down dough, place in center of flour and knead until dough is no longer wet, but not stiff. Shape into a round, flat disc. Grease or spray one (9-inch) cake pan. Place dough in center, cover with

O Pão

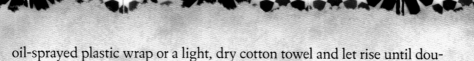

oil-sprayed plastic wrap or a light, dry cotton towel and let rise until doubled in bulk. Bake in 350°F oven 30 to 40 minutes or until golden. Internal temperature should reach 200°F on an instant-read thermometer; loaf will pull away from sides of pan; loaf sounds hollow when thumped.

*Some recipes use a blend of all-purpose and cake flour for an even lighter, finer crumb; ½ cup cake flour to 1½ cups all-purpose flour.

"It brought tears to my eye when you mentioned the fact that the Maui ladies bless their bread dough at the proper time (just before the loaf goes into the oven). My mother always did that.... She went to her grave with the knowledge that she was a terrific Portuguese bread maker. (Could play the 'ukulele and guitar well, also, but that's another story.)"

— *Dorothy Cataluna, Kaua'i, in a letter to me*

Pão Doce Peters
MRS. PETERS' SWEETBREAD (MODERNIZED)
Makes 2 loaves

The best-known of Portuguese breads in Hawai'i is pão doce, sweetbread. In the old days, it often was baked with a whole, unpeeled egg secreted within; the one who got the egg was believed to be blessed. I've updated this recipe from "the sweetbread lady," the late Alice Peters of the Big Island (page 175). She labeled it her "small recipe," but five pounds of flour may be a bit much unless yours is a powerful standing mixer. So you may have to do this the old-fashioned way, mixing by hand to form the dough, then kneading until you've lost the strength in your arms!

(continued on page 169)

For the yeast:
1 very small baking-type potato, peeled (or $\frac{1}{2}$ a large potato)
$\frac{1}{2}$ cup water
$\frac{1}{2}$ cup sugar
3 packets instant dry yeast (3 tablespoons)

For the dry mixture:
5 pounds bread flour (reserve 2 cups for kneading)
3 cups sugar
$\frac{1}{2}$ teaspoon salt

For the liquid mixture:
4 eggs
1 quart milk
2 blocks (1 cup) butter (she used Nucoa or Blue Bonnet
  margarine)
2 tablespoons vegetable shortening (I use butter-flavored)
$1\frac{1}{2}$ cups very hot water (not boiling but almost too hot to
  touch)
Butter-flavored spray or melted butter for rising process
Evaporated milk or egg wash

Make potato yeast starter: Grate or dice potato and place in a small pot
with water; bring to a boil, turn down heat and simmer until potatoes are
soft. Allow to cool to very warm (you can touch with finger); add sugar
and yeast. Allow to foam and bubble while assembling ingredients.

In the bowl of a standing mixer fitted with whisk or mixing paddle, mix
together flour, 3 cups sugar and salt. Change to dough hook. In a large
bowl, combine beaten eggs, milk or evaporated milk, butter slices, vegetable shortening and hot water. Stir well to melt butter and shortening.
Add liquid mixture to dry mixture gradually, beating with dough hook
until a smooth dough is formed, about 5 minutes.

(continued on the next page)

Sprinkle countertop with flour, place dough on counter and knead well, adding flour as needed. Small blisters should appear on the surface of the dough and, when pressed lightly with a finger, the dough should rise back to fill in the depression. The dough should feel light and moist, not clammy or stiff.

Spray a gigantic bowl with vegetable spray, or butter it. (In the absence of a large enough rising bowl, divide the dough in two before kneading and knead two pieces separately and place in 2 large bowls.) Place dough in bowl or bowls. Arrange a dry kitchen towel over and place in a warm, draft-free place to rise until doubled in bulk (60 to 90 minutes). Punch down dough, divide into two pieces, knead on a floured surface until light and puffy, forming into mounded rounds. Spray with butter-flavored spray or butter hands and run lightly over dough to coat. Let rise, covered with a dry kitchen towel, in warm place until doubled in bulk.

Preheat oven to 350°F. Place loaves in 9-inch pie pans, brush with egg wash or evaporated milk and bake at 350°F 40 to 50 minutes until deep golden brown, internal temperature reaches 190°F on instant-read thermometer and loaf sounds hollow when thumped. Cool on racks.

Variations: Add saffron threads to the liquid mixture for a bright yellow color. Add 1 tablespoon vanilla in place of 1 tablespoon of the milk. Add 2 teaspoons lemon extract. Add cinnamon or cinnamon and nutmeg or Portuguese 5-Spice—a teaspoon or two—to the dry ingredients.

Tip: A brief spelling lesson: In Portuguese, a single "s" makes a z sound; to achieve an "s" sound, you need a double "s." So, sorry Leonard's, it's malassadas.

PÃO DOCE

Lionel Medeiros was 65 and his baker-father, George Medeiros, had been making pão doce for the angels for many years when Lionel and I sat down at The Willows for a chat some years ago. But for Lionel, the scent of his father's crackling-crusted pão branco (plain white bread) lingered tantalizingly in memory.

George Medeiros, who died at age 85, had a long and eventful career. He was born here but raised in the Portuguese community of San Leandro, California. Then the family moved to Idaho, where they worked in the potato fields.

Returning to Hawai'i, he did his baking apprenticeship at the Alexander-Young Hotel, which then operated THE bakery in Honolulu. (For years, I at *The Advertiser* and Betty Shimabukuro at the then *Star-Bulletin* would receive pleading letters, almost tear-stained, begging for Alexander-Young recipes. But the recipes had died with the bakers.)

"He kept a leather book in his desk, of his recipes," Lionel recalled. "He didn't talk much and he didn't share those things."

In the late 1920s, Medeiros operated a self-named bakery on Harding Avenue between 10th and 11th Streets in Kaimuki; the family lived just up the street at 3405 Harding, Lionel recalled. (So many of my informants for this book recalled with distinct clarity their early addresses or four-digit phone numbers.)

Medeiros Bakery delighted customers with hand-wrapped loaves of pão, pão doce, pão de leite and other Portuguese standards. "He was the first baker in Kaimuki to make fresh bread, sliced and wrapped. Before, they had to go downtown to get that," Lionel said, proudly.

In 1939 or thereabouts, George Medeiros opened Colonial Bakery on Wai'alae Avenue, which he operated during WWII as best he could with rationing and regulations. But he received another challenge during the war, too. "In 1940 or thereabouts, he was contacted—I don't know why he was chosen—by the commander of the Navy mess hall at Pearl Harbor," Lionel said. George Medeiros began training enlisted men in bulk baking and helping the military equipment for a professionally equipped baker. He commuted back and forth once a week throughout the war, "doing his part," as they said then.

George Medeiros was an innovator and an early adapter. He invested in the latest mixers, sheeters and slicing machines. He created small paper tokens that people could buy when finances were flush and redeem over time for a given number of loaves of bread, like a primitive cash card or loyalty card.

But he was also cautious: "He never thought of expanding, of becoming a Love's," said Lionel, referring to the Hawai'i giant of bakeries. "He was very conservative. He didn't want to do anything where he would not have his hand right in it."

At the Alexander-Young, George Medeiros met and married Julia Cosme. Together, they had three children, two boys and a girl, with Lionel sandwiched in the middle.

Julia Cosme Medeiros spent years in the back of the bakery, wrapping bread in cellophane. "That was her specialty," Lionel said.

Lionel virtually grew up in the bakery; the bakers were his babysitters. It was his father's wish that he take over the business someday, though that never came to pass. He couldn't see himself, like his father, getting up at 3:30 every morning six days a week. His eyes misted as he recalled a recent visit to the site of his father's bakery; "the ovens are still there," he said, though he didn't specify where "there" was.

What he remembered most vividly is how much his father's breads differed from today's. Today, almost no one makes a plain white, Portuguese-style loaf anymore. Though the ingredients—yeast, water, flour, salt—resemble that of so-called French breads, the proportions, shaping and handling (the loves were round and mounded) were different.

And as to pão doce (sweetbread), "it was the old style, not this yellow, pasty stuff. It was white, white and hardened." Yellow food coloring never found its way into George Medeiros' pão doce, Lionel said. "Oh, NO!"

One Portuguese specialty Medeiros didn't make in his bakery was malassadas. "He got into malassadas at home. He would experiment with different kinds of ingredients. I liked everything he made. I haven't found anyone to match him," Lionel said.

When George Medeiros retired, he took with him two immense Hobart bread mixers. One, he gifted to chef John Peru and the other to Lionel. "They were so huge, you had to make bread for the whole neighborhood if you get them started," Lionel said.

He laughed, recalling his dad's home baking experiments. "He'd have trays all over the kitchen. My mother was a very typical Portuguese wife who would never complain. He would make one with more water, less flour, one at different temperatures."

Lionel sighed. "To this day, we miss him. Nobody could make bread like him."

Malassadas
PORTUGUESE DOUGHNUTS
Makes 5 dozen malassadas

Grandma never made malassadas. In fact, I don't know anyone who made them at home; they were (and are) bakery fare, county fair food, festa treats. Don't be nervous, though: If you can stir a dough and if you've ever made fried chicken or tempura, you're golden —and so are your doughnuts.

The keys are the same as for other deep-fried foods: doughnuts not over-large, fat at the right temperature, don't crowd, turn constantly as you fry, remove as soon as they're golden, drain on absorbent paper.

These ultra-rich and unusually shaped malassadas from Gregory Santos won first place in the Malassadas Recipe Contest sponsored by the Hawai'i Council on Portuguese Heritage at the February 1981 festa. Santos broke the no-hole malassadas rule: He poked the little pastries with a finger to assure the center would cook properly. (Mal assada means, literally, half-cooked or poorly cooked.)

1 teaspoon sugar
2 packages (2 tablespoons) dry yeast
1/3 cup very warm water
8 cups flour, sifted
1 cup sugar
1 teaspoon salt
1/2 cup (1 stick) butter, melted
6 whole eggs
7 egg yolks
1 1/3 cup evaporated milk
1 1/3 cups water
Vegetable oil for frying
Granulated sugar or sugar-cinnamon mixture

(continued on the next page)

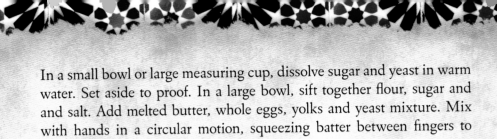

In a small bowl or large measuring cup, dissolve sugar and yeast in warm water. Set aside to proof. In a large bowl, sift together flour, sugar and and salt. Add melted butter, whole eggs, yolks and yeast mixture. Mix with hands in a circular motion, squeezing batter between fingers to incorporate.

In a bowl, blend evaporated milk and water. Add this to flour mixture, a little at a time, stirring with hands to mix. Place dough in an ungreased bowl, cover and place in warm draft-free place. Allow to rise until doubled in bulk, about 2 hours. Punch down and allow to rise again, about 30 minutes. Set aside.

Heat 3 inches oil in deep fryer or heavy-bottomed pot to 375°F on a candy thermometer. Test a small amount of dough; it should sizzle, puff up and brown within seconds without burning.

Pinch off balls of dough and roll into round. Using one finger, make a dent or hole in the ball. Drop 3 to 4 balls at a time in 375°F oil. Allow a crust to form, then quickly turn to prevent oil from soaking into the uncooked side. Continue turning as the malassadas cook.

Drain on paper towels and roll in sugar or sugar-cinnamon mixture. Serve hot.

O Pão

MRS. PETERS

Alice Peters

lice Lucas Peters was raised right. Not only did her mother teach her to bake, but Mrs. Lucas also taught her daughter not to talk stink.

So, when Mrs. Peters—"Auntie Alice" to a slice of the Hāmākua Coast—tasted my first attempt at duplicating her famous Portuguese sweetbread, she didn't actually blurt out, "You call this sweetbread?????"

She did wonder aloud if I'd used eggs. The color was pale, not the rich, eggy yellow she achieved with really fresh eggs.

"It's good," she said, very politely, "but a little dry, and you let it rise too long." (The loaf was the size of a manhole cover). Then she sweetly murmured, "I give you credit. At least you baked it. All my life I made. I like see somebody else make!"

I had brought bread to the baker, like coals to Newcastle, because Peters, then 93, suffered from various ailments including arthritis, and couldn't spend much time on her feet. With what I learned in that lively two-hour conversation, the sweetbread I've been making since I got home (see recipe, this section) bears no relation to that first, flawed attempt.

At one time, Alice Peters was among dozens of Portuguese women who made not-so-extra money baking bread for festive occasions, but also the daily loaf of crusty white or "milk" bread. These women used skills their mothers had learned in the Azores or Madeira to help support their families, even as they kept up with child-rearing and housework.

"No can help, eh? My husband's pay, plantation, was small. I didn't know how to make money because I couldn't go out to work (she had three young sons)," recalled Peters, who was born in Hilo in 1914, grew up in Kaiwiki, a plantation camp just to the Hāmākua side of Hilo, and married Levi A. Peters in 1937.

Casting about for a way to raise money, she recalled that her mother used to sell bread baked in the wood-burning forno. Inspired by that example, Peters began her baking career about 45 years ago, selling loaves out her back door.

In the 1960s or perhaps '70s—her normally sharp memory is vague about exactly what year—Peters and her late husband built the home that they would share for more than 30 years in the Pualoa section of Laupahoehoe. A short while later, to satisfy the health inspectors who had begun to crack down on off-the-books kitchen operations, Peters outfitted a bare-bones commercial kitchen in her home.

Wrapped in a big apron and with her hair tied up in a kerchief, Peters baked thousands of loaves for clubs and organizations to sell as fundraisers. There was no mixer; she beat and kneaded the dough by hand, babied the rising loaves by covering them with thin blankets, and kept multiple oil stoves going for hours, baking 11 loaves at a time.

Peters gave up the business only when her doctor threatened to tell her customers not to buy from her anymore. Even then, she continued to cook and bake in huge quantities for church fundraisers. Her handwritten personal cookbook included gargantuan recipes for chicken long rice, laulau and, of course, breads and her famous desserts.

Peters baked in batches of 100 or more loaves, starting with 65 pounds of flour, and she used an ungilded recipe: flour, sugar, salt, butter, eggs, yeast, milk. The only concession to modernity was that she didn't make yeast from a potato starter as her mother had done. But she did boost the power of commercial yeast with potato water.

In the old days, Peters said, "they were very, very strict" about how things should be done. Both her mother and her mother-in-law gave her grief about using commercial yeast and cooking with spices, but she just gently replied, "Mama, you cook your own, I cook my own."

Peters didn't romanticize the old days. Just as vividly as she recalled the crackling crust and tender crumb of bread baked in the forno, she also recalled swabbing the ashes out with rags tied to a broomstick. She hated it.

Just as she gratefully remembered how her baking efforts helped pay for the family home, so did she recall the last day of sixth grade, when she came home to tell her mother that she'd passed, and so would be able to go on to "the big school." "No," said her mother, "pau for you. You going work."

"I went through plenty," she said. "I went through plenty."

(Note: Mrs. Peters died in 2012.)

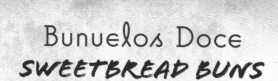

Buñuelos Doce
SWEETBREAD BUNS
Makes a couple of dozen rolls, depending on size

I owe Gerard Vincent a lot, though I doubt he remembers me. He lived in the same Kaʻaʻawa neighborhood as my brother and generously gave me the Portuguese cabbage plant from which my own is descended. He also gave me his treasured short-cut recipe for Sweetbread Buns. Mr. Vincent moved to Kauaʻi but I think of him often with affection.

10 cups flour (preferably high-gluten bread flour)
2 cups sugar
1½ teaspoons salt
2 teaspoons nutmeg
2 tablespoons active dry yeast
Butter-flavored spray
6 eggs, beaten
2 teaspoons lemon extract
1 cup evaporated milk, plus a little more for brushing
2 cups very warm water ("as hot as you can stand it")
1 cup (2 blocks) butter, softened

Combine dry ingredients in a large bowl and set aside. Spray vegetable oil spray on bottom and sides of a very large stainless steel bowl (mine is 16 inches across). Set aside.

In the bowl of a standing mixer, mix together wet ingredients and butter and add dry ingredients ½ cup at a time, mixing for about ½ hour. (Mr. Vincent uses a Kitchen Aid with a dough hook on Speed 2.) Transfer dough into prepared bowl and spray top of dough. Cover with damp kitchen towel and place bowl in refrigerator overnight; it will double in size.

(continued on the next page)

In the morning, punch down dough with floured hands on floured board and divide into even-sized balls to form buns. Place buns about 1 inch apart into butter-sprayed baking pans (9 x 13 or 11 x 17), you may need more than one. Let buns rise until touching. Brush tops of buns with evaporated milk.

Bake at 350°F for about 20 minutes, until nicely browned on top. Buns should sound hollow when tapped; internal temperature should reach 190°F.

Variation: Sweetbread rolls can be "stuffed" with haupia, or coconut pudding. Alice Peters of Laupahoehoe made haupia this way: Combine 2 cups fine, freshly shredded coconut, 2 teaspoons vanilla, 2 cups sifted powdered sugar, 4 tablespoons softened butter or margarine, a few drops of milk or cream or evaporated milk. You may add ½ cup raisins or chopped nuts. Bake the buns, split them and spread with the filling. Or form raw dough into flat rounds, put a dollop of haupia inside, pinch them into a ball and bake.

Pão de Leite
MILK BREAD
Makes 4 loaves

T his is an everyday bread harking back to the time when leaven-
ing was made from grated potatoes soakd in water, developing the
natural yeast. The mashed potatoes called for should be plain—no
butter or dairy. They are for texture, not flavor.

Half of a large baking potato, peeled and grated
½ cup warm potato water (recipe follows)
3 cups milk
1½ cups shortening
2 packages active dry yeast
1 cup sugar, divided
10 to 11 cups all-purpose flour, divided
1 tablespoon salt
1 cup mashed potatoes
Butter, shortening or oil spray for oiling the dough
Flour-oil spray for pans, if desired

To make potato water, place grated baking potato in ¾ cup water and
bring to a boil, simmering until potatoes are very soft and water is reduced to ½ cup. Reserve the grated potatoes. Scald milk (heat until small
bubbles form around the edge of the pot); stir in shortening until melted.

In a large bowl (preferably of a stand mixer, if you have one), dissolve
yeast in warm potato water, stir in ¼ cup sugar and the grated potatoes.
In a separate bowl, combine 8 cups flour with ¾ cup sugar and salt;
whisk together. Add the flour mixture and the mashed potatoes to the
yeast mixture; beat well with beaters or dough hook. Add milk alternately with enough of the remaining flour to make a stiff dough (some will be
left for the kneading process), mixing well with dough hook. In lieu of
a dough hook, turn out dough on a floured board and begin kneading.

(continued on the next page)

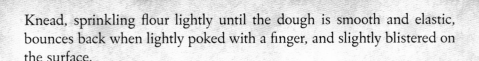

Knead, sprinkling flour lightly until the dough is smooth and elastic, bounces back when lightly poked with a finger, and slightly blistered on the surface.

Place dough in a large greased bowl, turning to grease top. Cover and rise in a warm place. Grease and flour four 9 x 5 x 3-inch loaf pans (or four round pie tins). On a lightly floured surface, divide dough into equal fourths. Shape each into a loaf or round. Cover lightly with a clean cotton kitchen towel and let rise until doubled. Preheat oven to 325°F. Bake for 45 minutes or until internal temperature reaches 200°F and loaves sound hollow when thumped.

Paozinhos
PORTUGUESE SANDWICH ROLLS
Makes 21 rolls

These crisp-outside, soft-inside "little breads" are a favorite else-where in the Portuguese world, though little known in the islands. It's another of my missions in life to see that these breads find a home here. They are perfect for piling with roasted or cured meats, cheeses, olive spreads, fish or egg salads, or for serving with soup or stew. Bake one batch at a time on the middle rack of your oven, preferably on shiny or dull gray pans; don't use your oldest, burnt-brown pans.

2 tablespoons active dry yeast
1 tablespoon sugar
1/2 cup very warm water
10 to 13 cups bread flour
4 cups warm water
1 tablespoon salt
1/2 cup solid shortening or butter-flavored solid shortening, melted
1/2 cup warm water
Shortening for greasing bowl
Evaporated milk for brushing

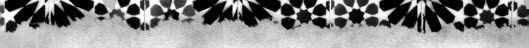

In a bowl or large measuring cup, combine yeast, sugar and very warm water. Allow to proof until doubled and bubbly. In a very large bowl, mix 8 to 9 cups flour with yeast mixture to make a "sponge" (a first rising), stir well, cover with cloth or dish towel and place in a warm place to rise until puffy (surface will be uneven and lumpy).

In a small bowl, combine salt, melted shortening and ½ cup water. Stir into batter and add 2 to 4 cups flour as you knead; turn out and knead a few minutes until dough is soft but not gluey. Poke the dough lightly, the depression should fill in and no dough should adhere to your poking finger. Clean bowl, rub with butter or shortening or oil-spray and place dough back in bowl. Cover with dish towel and allow to rise until doubled in bulk, about an hour.

Preheat oven to 475°F. Punch down dough, sprinkle with flour and knead briefly and pull off a generous ⅓ cup for each roll. Dip roll in flour and roll into round; flatten into disc and use the side of your hand to form a crease in the center of each roll. They will achieve a football shape. As they're made, place rolls on a kitchen towel, indented side down. Allow to rest 5 to 10 minutes. Place rolls on baking sheet or sheets indented side up, at least one inch apart. Brush with evaporated milk. Bake 10 minutes; check doneness. The rolls may take up to 15 minutes to become golden, crisp on the outside and tender on the inside.

Tip: Use paozinhos to make Prego No Pão, "Nailed Steak Sandwiches." Pound thinly sliced garlic into thin-cut or pounded steaks, then saute in olive oil with onion, red wine, salt and pepper. Stuff sandwiches with sliced steak.

PORTUGUESE BISCUITS
Makes 16 biscuits

The original recipe for these biscuits intrigued but appalled me, calling for 1 cup each of butter and sugar. Predictably, the result was heavy, overly sweet. Making the recipe over in a more conventional mode—more baking powder, a little salt, a solid shortening and drastically less sugar—resulted in the best biscuits I've ever made, rather rustic-looking, buttery with a nice balance of savory and sweet. Note: These biscuits do not keep well; eat them on baking day.

- **3 cups flour**
- **2 teaspoons baking powder**
- **2 tablespoons sugar**
- **1/4 teaspoon salt**
- **3 eggs**
- **1/2 cup butter-flavored Crisco**
- **1/4 cup soured milk, thin plain yogurt or whey from draining Greek yogurt**

Preheat oven to 350°F. Butter and flour or spray with oil-flour mixture, two (8- or 9-inch) round cake pans.

In a small bowl, whisk together flour, baking powder, sugar and salt.

In a large bowl, beat together eggs, Crisco and milk, yogurt or whey. Add the flour mixture in three additions, stirring in between.

Knead the mixture in a bowl—about 5 or 6, push-fold-turn movements—and allow to rest 10 minutes while you clean up.

Pull off about 2 tablespoons of dough, which will be a little wet and slightly puffy from the baking powder. Roll each into a sphere and place in prepared cake pan. Arrange rolls in a circle around the pan edge, leaving 3/4 inch between and placing one in the center. Bake 15 to 20 minutes until golden brown on top, 180°F internal temperature.

O Pão

Tip: To sour milk, place 1 teaspoon vinegar in 1 cup whole milk; this is also call "clabbering" the milk, it will thicken and clump a bit.

Tip: Many older Portuguese bread recipes call for lard or shortening; Butter-Flavored Crisco is a good compromise. Use it chilled or frozen for biscuits, melted when melted lard is called for.

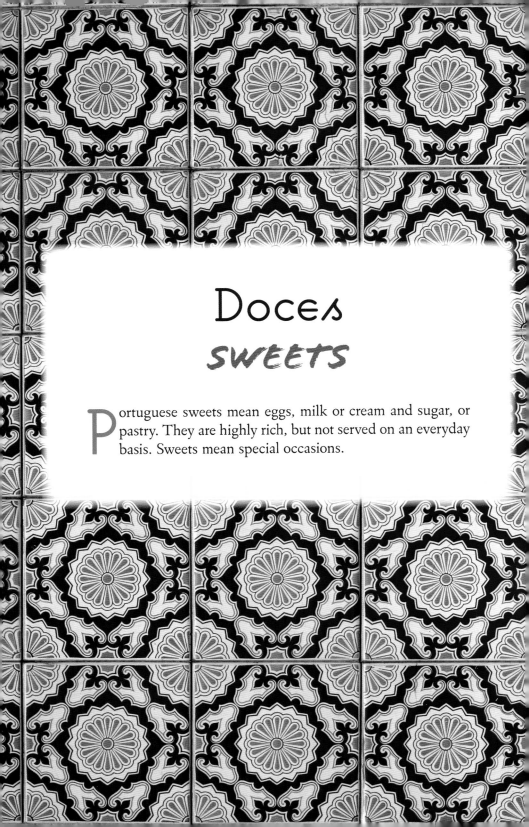

Doces

SWEETS

Portuguese sweets mean eggs, milk or cream and sugar, or pastry. They are highly rich, but not served on an everyday basis. Sweets mean special occasions.

PIPINELLAS PIE
Makes 8 to 10 servings

B aker Alice Peters of Laupahoehoe, whose cookies always sold out at fundraisers for her church, generously handed over her stained and handwritten recipes for a friend and me to copy.

Here's a pie you won't see every day—made from pipinellas, better known as chayote squash. Making these small, pear-shaped squash into a pie is rather like making quick bread from zucchini. In typical Portuguese fashion, the squash is embedded in an eggy custard.

    6 eggs, separated
    1¼ cups superfine ("baker's") sugar, or to taste
    6 cups pipinellas pulp*
    ½ teaspoon nutmeg
    1 teaspoon cinnamon
    1 teaspoon vanilla
    2 cups milk
    10 tablespoons cornstarch
    1 cup sugar
    1 single-crust pie shell, baked "blind"

In the bowl of a stand mixer, or with a hand-held mixer, beat egg whites until they hold soft peaks; still at high speed, gradually beat in add sugar to taste. Set aside.

Beat egg yolks, add pipenella pulp, nutmeg, cinnamon and vanilla and milk and stir well to combine. In a saucepan, whisk together cornstarch and sugar and slowly stir in milk in a steady stream. Cook over medium-low heat until thickened. Pour custard into pie crust. Scoop the meringue on top of the pie crust, flipping the rubber spatula a bit to make peaks. Bake at 325°F for 20 to 30 minutes until peaks are lightly browned.

* For pulp, peel pipinellas (a fussy chore) with vegetable peeler. Chop into chunks, then process briefly in food processor, pulsing on and off until pulpy but not liquefied.

Pudim Flan
PORTUGUESE BURNT CREAM
Makes 8 to 10 servings

This version of Burnt Cream requires a flan pan: a straight-sided, deep, oven-proof baking dish. Or use a high-sided 8-inch cake pan or even a deep-dish pie pan, although the sides will slope. The flan is baked in a bain marie (water bath) with caramel on the bottom, then overturned so the caramel is on top. Depending on the depth of your pan, you may not have room for all the custard; use the extra in individual ramekins.

> 1³/₄ cups sugar, divided
> 8 eggs
> 1 quart milk
> 3-inch length cinnamon stick
> 1¹/₂ teaspoons vanilla

Preheat oven to 350°F. In a small, heavy skillet, melt ³/₄ cup sugar over medium heat; do not stir. Cook 4 to 5 minutes, lifting the pot every half-minute to swirl until sugar is light brown and caramelized. Quickly pour this syrup into a deep 6-cup flan pan; tilt to coat bottom and sides evenly. Cool. In a saucepan, heat milk and cinnamon stick just to scalding (small bubbles appear around the rim). Discard cinnamon stick. Allow milk to cool to lukewarm. In a large bowl of electric mixer, beat eggs; gradually add remaining 1 cup sugar. Stir milk slowly into egg mixture; add vanilla. Pour milk mixture gently and slowly over caramel. Place flan pan in deep baking pan and fill outer pan with hot water to ¹/₂ inch below the top of the flan pan, cake or pie pan. Bake 1 hour or until a knife inserted halfway between center and edge of pan comes out clean; chill thoroughly. To serve, loosen edges with knife; invert onto serving dish. Spoon any caramel syrup that remains in pan over flan.

GUAVA JAM SQUARES
Makes 12 to 16 servings, depending on bar size

H ere's another from baker Alice Peters: jam squares. She made these with guava jam, topped with coconut and corn flakes. I dropped the corn flakes but kept the coconut.

Nonstick vegetable oil spray
1½ cups unbleached all-purpose flour
1¼ cups quick-cooking oats
⅓ cup granulated sugar
⅓ cup brown sugar
¼ teaspoon salt
¼ teaspoon baking soda
½ cup nuts (walnuts, pecans or almonds), finely chopped
12 tablespoons unsalted butter, cut into 12 pieces, softened but still cool
1 cup guava jam (NOT jelly, and preferably homemade jam)
½ cup angel-flake sweetened coconut

Adjust oven rack to lower-middle position. Preheat oven to 350°F. Spray 8- or 9- inch square baking pan with nonstick cooking spray. Fold two 16-inch lengths of foil lengthwise to measure 8 inches wide. Fit one into bottom of greased pan, pushing into corners and up sides, leaving overhang for handles. Press second sheet into pan, in the same manner, but perpendicular to the first sheet. Spray with nonstick spray.

In the bowl of a standing mixer, stir together flour, oats, sugars, baking, soda, salt and nuts on low speed. With mixer still on low speed, add butter pieces; continue to beat until mixture is well-blended and resembles wet sand, about 2 minutes.

Scrape ⅔ of the mixture into prepared pan and pat down evenly with hands or spatula. Bake 20 minutes, until starting to brown. Meanwhile, blend coconut into remaining oat-nut mixture. When the base has start-

(continued on the next page)

ed to brown, open the oven and using oven mitts and a rubber spatula, spread preserves evenly over hot bottom crust. Sprinkle coconut-crumb mixture evenly over jam. Bake until jam bubbles around edges and top is golden brown, about 30 minutes, rotating pan from front to back halfway through. Cool on wire rack to room temperature, about an hour, then remove from pan using foil handles. Cut into squares.

BROTHER/SISTER ORANGE COOKIES
Makes 40 cookies

These are a version of the cookies known variously as Russian Tea Cakes, Mexican Wedding Cookies, Melting Moments, Italian Butternuts... But in Portugal, oranges and pine nuts, rather than vanilla and walnuts, add interest to this simple cookie. Proportion—butter to sugar to flour—is all-important. My first attempts weren't so hot until I called on the family expert—Younger Brother (step-brother), who is half-Russian—and just a bit of tinkering made magic.

1 cup cool, slightly softened butter, sliced
1/2 cup sifted powdered sugar
Zest of 1 orange
1 teaspoon orange extract
2 1/2 cups sifted all-purpose flour
1/4 teaspoon salt
1 (2.5-ounce) package pine nuts

Preheat oven to 400°F. Spray or grease two cookie sheets, preferably shiny aluminum.

In a standing mixer or large mixing bowl with a hand-held mixer, cream together butter and sugar. Add zest and extract and beat in. Beat in sifted flour and salt. Remove from mixer when a soft dough forms; stir in pine nuts.

Using a miniature ice cream scoop or melon baller, pull up a knob of dough and roll into a short, blunt-ended log.

Place on center rack and bake at 400°F for 9 minutes; bottoms will be deep golden, tops will be light golden brown. Keep careful track of time. Place on a rack.

Place a cup or so of sifted confectioners' sugar in a flat plate or bowl and, while cookies are still warm, carefully roll them in confectioners' sugar or spoon sugar over. Cover thoroughly. Place on a rack to cool. Cool completely and store in airtight container. Serve within a few days.

MALASSADA BREAD PUDDING
Makes 8 to 10 servings

hen you have leftover malassadas, do as my friend Stephanie Rezents does: Freeze them and use them to make bread pudding. Each Leonard's-size malassada, chopped, amounts to about a cup of bread chunks. Use your favorite recipe but bake at 350°F for 65 minutes. Or try my approach. (I don't like raisins in my bread pudding, but you could add ½ cup.)

> **6 cups stale malassadas, torn or chopped**
> **Softened butter for baking dish**
> **3 cups nonfat half-and-half or whole milk**
> **4 eggs**
> **½ cup unsalted butter, melted**
> **½ cup brown sugar, packed**
> **2 teaspoons vanilla**
> **2 teaspoons Portuguese 5-Spice or Pumpkin Pie Spice**

Place malassadas in large buttered casserole or 9 x 13 baking dish; the pieces should be smallish, not big chunks. In a bowl, blend together non-fat half-and-half, eggs, butter, brown sugar, vanilla and spices. Pour mixture over malassadas, covering evenly. Press bread under liquid. (If mixture seems dry, stir in ½ cup additional half-and-half or milk.) Let stand for 30 minutes or more. (You can stop at this point, cover and refrigerate overnight, if desired.)

Preheat oven to 350°F. Place the casserole or baking pan in another pan (your oven roasting pan works for this) and fill that pan with hot water until it comes halfway up the sides of the bread pudding dish. Bake 60 to 65 minutes, until bread pudding is set and not soupy.

Biscoitos de Nogueira
GLAZED WALNUT SQUARES
Makes 9 to 12 squares, depending on size of cut

These bar cookies are cake-like, rich and moist. If you choose the Madeira-flavored glaze, the tops will be a lovely pinkish purple color but awfully sweet. I prefer just a brush of wine.

- **6 tablespoons flour**
- **$\frac{1}{2}$ teaspoon baking powder**
- **$\frac{1}{2}$ cup butter, softened**
- **$\frac{1}{2}$ cup firmly packed light brown sugar**
- **1 egg, lightly beaten**
- **2 tablespoons milk**
- **2 tablespoons Madeira wine**
- **$\frac{1}{2}$ teaspoon vanilla**
- **1 cup walnuts, finely chopped (reserve 1 tablespoon for garnish)**
- **Glaze (recipe follows)**

Spray a 9 x 9-inch baking dish with oil-flour baking spray or butter and flour it in the old-fashioned way. Preheat oven to 350°F. In a medium mixing bowl, combine flour and baking powder; set aside. In a standing mixer or using a hand-held mixer in a large bowl, cream together butter and sugar until light and fluffy. Beat in egg. Add milk, 2 tablespoons of the wine and the vanilla. Gradually stir flour into creamed mixture. Stir in walnuts, reserving a tablespoon or so for garnish. Spread in prepared baking pan. Scatter walnut garnish over. Bake in 350°F oven for 15 to 20 minutes. While cookie is still hot, brush top with remaining wine. Cool and glaze, if desired. When glaze is set, use a pointed, serrated knife to cut into squares.

Variation: Omit glaze; brush warm cake with 2 tablespoons additional Madeira. (I prefer this to the glaze as this recipe is amazingly sweet already.)

Plain or lemon glaze: To make a matching glaze that hardens quickly, beat together 2 tablespoons Madeira or port, 2 tablespoons water and 3 cups sifted powdered sugar. For lemon glaze, combine the zest of two lemons and juice of 2 lemons with 3 cups sifted powdered sugar.

PORTUGUESE ALMOND CAKE
Makes 12 servings

This recipe, published in The Honolulu Advertiser *in 1973, is said to have come from the Algarve, the gift of a Moorish king to his homesick wife, who missed almonds. Typical of many Portuguese sweets, it is based on a sugar syrup into which egg yolks are slowly stirred. It takes some care, but if you are patient and don't allow the custard to boil, you'll be just as charmed as the queen must have been. Note: This cake requires an 8-inch tart pan with a removable bottom.*

1½ cups almonds
1 teaspoon softened butter or butter spray
1½ cups sugar
⅓ cup water
8 egg yolks
1 teaspoon almond extract
¾ teaspoon cinnamon

Preheat oven to 350°F. Blanch almonds: Bring to a boil a large pot of boiling water; remove from heat and pour almonds in. After 1 minute (time yourself!), drain almonds; rinse under cold water to stop cooking. Then squeeze each almond between thumb and forefinger and it will pop right out of its skin.

Scatter almonds on a cookie sheet and toast 10 minutes at 350°F. Remove almonds to cool. Raise temperature to 400°F. Process almonds in food processor, pulsing on and off, to fine crumbs. Butter or spray tart pan with butter spray. Sprinkle with 2 tablespoons of the sugar.

Combine 1¼ cups of sugar and water in a saucepan (you'll have 2 tablespoons left for later use). Bring to a boil, stirring until sugar dissolves. Add almonds and cook over medium heat, stirring constantly, five minutes. Remove from heat and cool slightly.

(continued on the next page)

In a bowl, beat egg yolks well. Gradually, in a thin stream, begin beating egg yolks into saucepan of sugar-almond syrup. Add almond extract and cinnamon, stirring well. Reduce heat to medium-low and return to heat; stir until mixture thickens, about 10 minutes. Do not allow to boil. When thickened (like hot pudding instead of thin cream). Pour mixture into prepared pan, sprinkle with remaining 2 tablespoons sugar and bake 15 minutes.

ELEANORA CADINHA'S FRUITCAKE
Makes 2 to 3 loaves

At 85, my mother has stopped baking her fruitcake; I've got her last loaf in the freezer and can't make myself eat it because I know I'll never have it again. So perhaps next holiday season, I'll make this one, treasured by former Hawaiian Electric cooking demonstrator Eleanora Cadinha.

For the fruits:
1 pound glazed fruits
1 pound dates, chopped
1 pound raisins
½ cup molasses
½ cup sherry

For the cake:
4 cups walnuts, coarsely chopped
1 cup butter, softened
1¼ cups brown sugar, packed
4 eggs
2 cups flour
¼ teaspoon baking soda
¼ teaspoon salt
½ cup teaspoon ground cloves
½ teaspoon mace
1 teaspoon cinnamon

In a large bowl, combine fruits, sherry and molasses. Allow mixture to stand for a week, stirring several times (this ages the fruit and improves the flavor of the cake). Note: This has traditionally been done at room temperature, but if you aren't comfortable with that, place the fruit in the refrigerator.

Preheat oven to 275°F. Add walnuts to the fruit mixture and mix well. In a large bowl, cream butter and brown sugar until light and fluffy. Add eggs one at a time and blend well after each addition. In a separate bowl, sift dry ingredients three times and add to creamed mixture. Add fruits. Stir well. Bake in 2 large or 3 medium loaf pans. Decorate with additional fruit, if desired. Line pans with waxed paper and then with greased kitchen parchment or heavy brown paper. Place a pan of water on the lower rack or bottom of the oven. Bake at 275°F for 2½ hours. Remove cake from pan and cool thoroughly before removing paper. Leave the waxed paper on. Trim uneven edges and wrap in foil. Store in a cool place or freeze.

GRANDMA'S COCONUT TURNOVERS

Coconut turnovers were a centerpiece pastry of my childhood. If we weren't eating Grandma's, we were buying them at Nashiwa or Yokouchi bakeries. Now we go to Home Maid Bakery, Sam Sato's, or make these.

> ½ cup sweetened condensed milk
> 3 cups fresh coconut (NOT sweetened flaked coconut), grated
> 1 to 2 teaspoons cornstarch
> 1 recipe unbaked double-crust pastry (homemade, refrigerated or from a mix)

Preheat oven to 375°F. Blend together condensed milk and coconut; sprinkle cornstarch into mixture and stir to incorporate. Roll pastry out and cut into 4-inch circles. Place about 2 tablespoons of coconut mixture just off center on each circle. Fold pastry into a semicircle and use a fork to depress edges together.

Double-crust pie crust: In the bowl of a standing mixer, combine 4 cups all-purpose flour, 2 teaspoons salt, 1 tablespoon sugar; chill the entire bowl. Cut one pound very cold butter into 8 slices per stick; keep refrigerated until use. In standing mixer on low speed mix chilled flour/salt/sugar; add butter one piece at a time until broken into bean-size pieces. Drop by drop, add up to ⅔ cup ice water; until dough comes together, forming a ball. Wrap dough in plastic wrap and chill 1 hour. Then you're ready to roll.

Delicia de Laranja
ORANGE PUDDING
Makes 10 to 12 dessert servings

Citrus, sugar, eggs: It's got to be a Portuguese dessert! I've made this twice; the first time it separated as it chilled, but it was still delicious. The second time it worked beautifully. The difference between the two experiences: Patience. Fifteen minutes is a long time when you're stirring.

> **4 envelopes plain gelatin**
> **Juice of 4 fresh oranges**
> **Zest of 4 oranges**
> **2 cups sugar**
> **2 quarts whole milk, room temperature**
> **24 large eggs, separated**
> **12 tablespoons confectioners' sugar**

In a bowl, sprinkle gelatin over orange juice. In a saucepan, combine gelatin-orange mixture, orange rind and sugar. Stir until dissolved. In a large bowl, beat egg yolks lightly; add milk, then stir yolks into milk along with gelatin. Pour into a large saucepan with a bottom the same size as the burner. Place heat on medium-low and cook, stirring constantly, 15 to 20 minutes, until slightly thickened, like a thin custard sauce. Do not allow mixture to boil and do not stop stirring or the bottom will thicken but not the top. Transfer to a large bowl.

In another large bowl, beat egg whites to soft peaks, then gradually add confectioners sugar, folding it in. Gently but thoroughly fold beaten egg whites into orange mixture. Pour into large bowl or individual serving dishes and chill 24 hours. Serve cold with crisp butter cookies or wafers (gaufrettes).

Tip: Folding is not stirring. To fold in a whipped mixture, push the flavored mixture to one side of the bowl, or tilt the bowl so the flavored mixture slides over. Spoon in about 1/3 of the whipped whites, then, using a rubber spatula, lift the whites up, over and under the flavored mixture. Stirring breaks down the trapped bubbles in the egg white. Work slowly until incorporated; a few streaks of white are OK.

APPENDICES

INDEX

ABOUT THE AUTHOR

Wanda Adelaide Adams, a Portuguese-American "Keiki O Kepaniwai" ('Īao Valley, Maui) learned to love reading from her mother, the family's first college graduate. She inherited the love of newsprint from her printer grandfather. From her Southern father, she absorbed storytelling. And from her grandmother, cooking. These produced a 40-year career in newspapers, freelancing, writing and editing cookbooks. Her first cookbook, *The Island Plate Recipes and Food Lore from 150 Years of The Honolulu Advertiser* was a bestseller. She's at work on a sixth book (not telling yet!). She lives in Kalihi with her high school sweetheart, two cats, a prolific fig tree and every kitchen tool known to man.

With the exception of the "Variations on a Portuguese Theme" chapter, the photographs for this book were taken at Leeward Community College with the enthusiastic assistance of students from an Asian/continental cuisine class at LCC. The students tested the recipes and prepared each dish for its moment in the spotlight. Many thanks to chef-instructor David Millen, whose efficiency and wealth of knowledge kept us on track each day.

OTHER COOKBOOKS
BY MUTUAL PUBLISHING

To order these titles and more, visit
www.mutualpublishing.com